REMAINS

Stories of Vietnam

REMAINS

Stories of Vietnam

By William Crapser

Sachem Press Old Chatham, New York

Published by Sachem Press, P.O. Box 9, Old Chatham, NY 12136.

Printed in the United States of America.

All characters in this book are fictional. Any resemblance to actual persons, living or dead, is purely coincidental.

Library of Congress Cataloging-in-Publication Data

Crapser, William
Remains: stories of Vietnam.

1. Vietnamese conflict, 1961-1975--Fiction.
I. Title.
PS3553.R2737R4 1988 813'.54 88-6667
ISBN 0-937584-13-4
ISBN 0-937584-14-2 (pbk.)

In loving memory of

Private First Class William M. Bagshaw
"H" Company, 2nd Battalion, 5th Marines
1st Marine Division
September 16, 1949 - February 26, 1968
killed in action, Hue City, Vietnam

Lieutenant Wilfred Owen
"D" Company, 2nd Battalion, Manchester Regiment
March 18, 1893 - November 4, 1918
killed in action, Sambre Canal, France

"I weep for Adonais—he is dead!"
—Shelley

Contents

Prologue 1

I Dream What I Am (poem) 3

The Descent 4

The War Enters 9

The Wall:Michael Bowle 11

Proud 13

New Man 19

Baptism of Fire 21

Hungers 27

A Letter Home 35

A Letter Home 37

Billy Sunday 39

Education of a Pointman 44

Nicky Martinez 49

R&R 58

A Letter Home 71

Battle Survivor (poem) 73

For Timothy Baer 74

The Rest 81

Remains 83

A Letter Home 91

Remains (poem) 95

Land of the Free, Home of the Brave 96

Wild Child 102

Let It Be 165

Ceremony of the Beast (poem) 170

Epilogue 172

PROLOGUE

Though it was a small war, Vietnam was as close as we will get to a modern conventional conflict. The future wars will, like Vietnam, be without boundary or definition. A place where heroes no longer exist. Only the dead and their survivors. Only the psychotic "sane" warriors and their "insane" frightened followers.

A place of killing only, where insanity will become the only escape on the battlefield. There will be no other way, and I can offer no explanation beyond trying to survive it.

It will be the misled trying to lead. It will be boys trying to die like men.

There is no religion, no god in war. No leader, shaman, priest, philosopher, poet or prophet who can stand up in the middle of withering enemy fire, raise his hand and give meaning or heal the slaughter. He will go down. He will go down screaming "Corpsman! Corpsman!" just like everybody else. There are no masks you can wear in war.

The grunt, the infantryman, saw the last of his kind in Vietnam. He no longer exists as a viable fighting force.

Now, in a modern conventional war, with the killing power of weapons systems, there will be immense numbers of dead, with no military superiority or victory on either side. A war waged by chemically-induced psychopaths taking killing to staggering heights, ensuring mutual suicide for all opposing forces. They are working on the chemical now. It will block out the combatant's fear, his humanity, and he will calmly fight with ruthless abandon to his death. Those who refuse to take the drug will become psychiatric casualties within the first day, perhaps even hours or minutes.

Now, in a modern conventional war, one can expect two or three million casualties in the first two or three days of fighting on any major front!

Within a week the number of dead will equal that of a nuclear attack. A week of conventional war or a day of the bomb. This has become our last, marginal choice. And with advanced technology they are fast closing even that gap. Nuclear war is no longer the deterrent it once was. Conventional war and the bomb are fast approaching equality on this tiny cinder of a planet.

We must never fight again!

It is over for the heroic, individual fighting man.

The end of the grunt has come.

In Vietnam you will find the last of his remains.

I DREAM WHAT I AM

I dream what I am, a self
That's orbiting, symbolic, alive.
I see a child warrior's tears
Freeze in the nights, knowing
I winter there.

I hold three numbers in my hand.
Earth, Spirit, and Time.
They add and subtract me.

Earth, the light I walk on
Buried beneath my stone with the soiled
Heart, bursting down arteries
To the dark destinations of blood.
In fire and love. Our infinite embrace.

Spirit, the dice I roll
With these high stakes.
Watching my shadow shaken
In the hands of a gambler
And tossed in a rattle of bones
Against the inscrutable walls.
Trying to break even.

Time, the eyes moving on, trying to disguise me.
Older, I turn the hands of all my clocks upward
Trying to find me.

Earth, Spirit, and Time.
I winter there.
They add and subtract me.
In fire and love. Our infinite embrace.
Trying to break even.
Trying to find me.

The Descent

Prepare yourselves, people, for the descent...
1968
The specter of these clouds in a darkening sky—
hammers held in fists balled and blackened.
At Parris Island, South Carolina, young warriors train.
The Drill Instructors shout
"Don't be afraid to bleed, shitheads! Blood's good for the grass! Blood makes the grass grow!"
The young warriors smile...Wolf blood surges through their veins...With ruthless snarls they attack the obstacle course...
Nothing stops them...The DIs shout "Move, pukes, move! Become strong! There's fightin' an' dyin' waitin' for ya! Ya don' wanna waste time!"
Young warriors lunge with their bayonets...
Taut muscles that only a month before held a young girl near grow tauter, tighter, angrier...
On the rifle range the young warriors think nothing of young girls...
The bull's eye, sir, never wanna miss!...
They began there, with a weapon in his hands, to show him respect...
Plenty of good food, a John Wayne movie...
They honed the edge there...
They gave him the final stanza of the "Marine Corps Hymn"...
An expert rifleman's badge...
And sent him to war in Vietnam.
The two weeks leave at home were strange...
"Strange days are on us...strange days have tracked us down..."
He listened closely to the song...The Doors...already leading the truth of him toward the rebellion...
He left early for final training in California...
Already he felt different...Already he only wanted to be with his

buddies who suffered the Parris Island heat and training...

He received word that his best friend was killed in Hue City...
The Tet offensive...
Listening to the Stones' "Citadel" he watched the wounded warriors return...Young men graduated from Parris Island only a month before him are torn, haggard, aged beyond repair...
"They murdered us over there! The Citadel Walls, never forget...The Citadel Walls!"
Yes, brother, the Citadel, the young warrior escorted his best friend's body home...

When that silver coffin came home on that silver American Airlines jet, that's when my life changed forever. Riding it back to the funeral parlor I touched the cold grey silver of it. My friend, my brother, you are home. Only a month ago we visited another friend in the same room where you now lie draped with a strange flag. I must identify you. I will see you one last time. The funeral director says you're vacuum-sealed and we have to be careful and pull the right latch. A loud click. Like the hood of a car, the lid opens a few inches. The smell of flowers is thick. I reach and lift open the lid. There, under plate glass, from the waist up, in Marine dress blue uniform, you lie. Looking old, broken nose, dried blood on blond hair, slight fuzz of whiskers on chin and cheek. Drawn, gone, beyond repair. I saw America under that lid, stretched in the heavy metal coffin, dried blood on blond hair. The Statue of Liberty shed tears the day we buried you. And then toppled into the sea. The country shook, like some vast earthquake were breaking it up. Day and night I sat silently by your coffin. Day and night I waited for the burial of America.

The March day we took you to the cemetery dawned bright with a cold, brisk wind. As your coffin settled on straps over the yawning hole of time's endless grave, of war's endless pit, of America's dying, I picked a few maple leaves and dropped them into the lead outer container already placed at the bottom, open, waiting. As I walked away, bugles played Taps, and I heard the persistent sound of guns. Seven men, three times in unison raised rifles to the sky and shot them toward God. KA-blame...I jumped...KA-blame...I shivered...KA-blame...I walked away finally from the burial of America.

The tears shed will have to be shed so many times over the sea will never open again to show the Statue of Liberty or her tears or the height the torch once held.
Rage into the night and all the nights to come. Rage an anger so deep. The pit of the feeling is the grave, yawning, omnipotent, waiting.

I must fight now, I must go to war. I must do battle with the enemy that has buried America. Nothing will make sense. I will be hated by one side, despised and ignored by the other. The months that follow are kaleidoscope-like, vast, all-encompassing. Sheer terror through nights so thick only death will penetrate with the sharp detonations of presence. I will be shot at and I will kill.

A revulsion raises itself, a masked vileness, like a bile that twists my stomach and knots my mind. Rage, goddammit, rage! At the piles of bodies for nothing. Rage at the killing! Rage an anger so deep maybe America will rise from the dead!

let the hands pound these words as need be to full explode vietnam war struggle lead aching heart torn soul madness through entrails dry and sticky on dirt road by mudder's ridge flies buzzing down to grab what they want full once again on vietnam's most abundant crop fly off to digest and wait for the next course which is on the way always on the way always...

where was I praying to lead through this terrible pain gnawing somewhere if seen truthfully there the wound by its very presence brings weight to history brings to wind and swaying time a perpetual undestroyable eulogy to the vietnam dead gives perpetual undestroyable eulogy to the returning warriors who can never shake it can never let seem to relax let muscles and body and mind just cool it for a while tight bound bitter angry no matter where this journey leads me has led everyone may lead all of us let now be known no matter what the vision this written history here coming forward...

i was fighting no dying no let it rip free verse style gotta blow true to the notes that's heard absurdity upon absurdity mounts itself powerful wall-like around my consciousness let the flow flow brother don't be afraid of what's seen let it rip rock and roll

o i scream twenty years later o i scream consumed in the night by the face's exploding flesh splattering grass brain tissue never to carry any image but that of the flies the persistent hungry flies of war a war that made no sense i am a hero of madness a hero who can't sleep nightmares the wound the wound where is the wound brother in the night i only hear your groan and your curse to god! i feel your body for blood there's blood on my hands everywhere i touch somehow the flow of blood must be stopped a voice help me help me not spoken but worthed help me help me what have i done blood covers everything! blood sun blood moon blood ground blood mouth they're coming through! o shit! so dark! i can't see! explosions rock the air suck the air from my lungs! deafen me! what am i doing here! i'm running out of ammo! still hours before dawn! o how much more blood! jackson hit johnson hit corpsman blew away wasted let it end somehow two magazines left for my rifle i'm so very tired i just want to sleep please in the descent could i please just sleep away a while this unbelievable that took place this absurdity after twenty years can i not sleep without the flies and the dry remains and the faces that never die

"What passing-bells for these who die as cattle?
Only the monstrous anger of the guns."
—Wilfred Owen

"They shall rest from their words
And take their works with them."
—Ecclesiastes

The War Enters

The war enters in Vietnam, where a peasant in a small thatched hut prays peacefully before his altar. Burning incense and enchanting the gods of life and love, nature and nurturing, seed-time and blossom.

Suddenly, someone kicks in the door. It is dark except for the amber points of incense burning and the sound of his prayers.

The attacker is a Vietcong sympathizer, and she drives the bayonet on her rifle straight for his heart. She is part of an assassination squad sent to kill him.

In the deep abyss of his fear, the peasant parries the thrusts, overcomes her, and chokes her to death. He takes her rifle and shoots her. He feels her face, knows she is a woman. The peasant starts sobbing and begins to chant again.

The rifle shot stirs commotion outside, and in moments the door bursts open. The peasant, in a reflex of despair, raises the rifle, sees a rifle in another's hands, and fires three more shots. A man falls dead by the first. They lie before his altar.

The peasant lights some candles that cast a halo over each of the faces. One, the face of a dead woman, a Viet Cong. One, the face of a dead man, a United States Marine.

The blood reaches the base of the altar. The peasant sits silent before it.

Then, the door is opened slightly by the toe of a boot, and something is thrown in. The peasant does not look.

Was it thrown by a man or a woman? Of his land or against his land? For humanity or against humanity? He could not stop it.

The warriors who walk in. Does it matter? They are Viet Cong and North Vietnamese men and women. They are United States Marines. They find three bodies. A shattered altar. Fragmented religious artifacts.

When they leave, they torch the hut and calmly watch the flames consume it. The war moves on.

The Wall: Michael Bowle

The war raged around me. Sporadic bursts of gunfire came from the far shore, across the swollen river. Staccato bursts drilled the air only a hundred meters from my position. I thought if I could make it to the river, I would be safe, for the night at least. The war had circumnavigated me, as if I were the world, and I gasped in its strangling.

I was only trying to make it home.

The firing was thickest from the buildings directly across from me. Rapid fires, a slim silence, then rapid fires again.

A ferocious explosion burst in my brain! I was nauseous where I lay blown against a high, dark wall. "Move! Move!" my mind screamed. But my body made no reply. The concussive echoes of more rockets rushed through with loud hushes.

I've been in the war only four days. Someone told me this place is called "Way City."

There must be bodies all over now, littering the streets. The ones I've seen were covered with black flies. Black flies are war's symbol of nourishing. Maggots churn in heat through the whole body, wriggling in chests that quiver, as though the corpses were alive. Twisting in their silence, waiting.

The sun set and I knew with darkness the battle would increase. The concussion was wearing off, but my hands and feet were numb, my head ringing.

I kept my right finger on the trigger of my rifle, my left hand steadying it with a sweaty grip. Visions in my head multiplied faster and faster, the actions and scenarios in which my life and death would instantly be played out, step by step.

I moved along the dark wall with a heightening awareness reaching hysteria, but I didn't cry out.

The tempo of the battle increased. Staccato machine guns

traced their fast flight across the ground, impacting rounds searching for me. Explosions, shots, and rockets were reaching an ear-wrenching crescendo.

A cataclysmic attack began. In the center of the city, reaching like a long line, red and orange fire rolled toward me. The huge detonations ripped along in flashes, blood-red, dark crimson, white heat, bruised blue, black smoke billowing out, the splays of fiery color raced through.

I pressed myself against the wall. My head was in a thousand concussions at once. Men erupted, twisted and singed by the instantaneous surrealism of war. The reality of the surreal that lives and feels and dies in the smallest instant of time, and tears forever this life into its grotesque quotations. It is the moment the maggots inherit the earth.

Stretched out along the dark wall by the brutality of our acts as a people, as a nation. Rotting in our knowledge, rotting in our teaching, rotting in our judgment.

Did anyone learn last night?

Did anyone win?

I was only trying to make it home.

PROUD

I arrived in 'Nam Sunday and it's now Thursday. I flew out of Norton Air Force Base in California, refueled in Hawaii, then on to Okinawa. Stayed a few days there storing sea-bags, then climbed on a commercial airliner for the run to DaNang. We refueled on Wake Island. They flew me in a C-130 cargo plane from DaNang to Phu-Bai. I spent the night and flew the next day from Phu-Bai to Dong-Ha. Then I caught a truck convoy up to Camp Carroll, a long ride, man!

We passed the outskirts of Quang-Tri City, then swung east along Route 9 toward Cam-Lo Ville, and on past "Disneyland North," a Navy Sea-bee camp, and on up to Camp Carroll.

Everything here shimmers.

They halted the column in Cam-Lo for about an hour, and two mamasans came by our truck, pulled up their blouses and showed their tits. The marines in the truck whistled. The mamasans were old and their eyes seemed to be putting a spell on me. I felt weird. One of them looked at me, squatted, and pissed in the street, laughing up at me all the time, her teeth black from chewing betel nut. Betel nut makes them high. They seem to be high all the time. I'm always wondering what they're thinking.

They loaded my truck up front with ice cream for the grunts. Twelve huge round containers. I spent the ride watching vanilla and chocolate ice cream melt in the heat, ooze out of the containers like a wound, and stream around my new jungle boots and out the back of the truck in a steady, thick dripping. In the heat and dust I felt my mind was melting, the whole experience, my eyes seeing black and white, the thickness of the being, pouring out from their own containers of bodies, black on one side, white on the other. Then, reaching my boots, blending thick and sticking, steadily staining all that was lost on every inch of this road.

Along the road, Vietnamese had little stands set up where they sold beer and whiskey. The beer's called "tiger piss," and the grunts don't like it. Usually each stand had a couple of bottles sitting in front of two or three patient sellers. These stands were all along Route 9, popping up through the arid valley where no villes were in sight. Everywhere I looked around me I saw shell craters. All different sizes, ours and theirs, and the people so calm it's frightening.

I saw a bottle of Seagrams 7 and Canadian Club at one stand, but a big black grunt, his jungle fatigues bleached white from the bush in the heat and the sun, wearing a North Vietnamese Army belt buckle, a big red star on it, stopped me from buying. He said, almost fatherly, explaining this quietly, that the Vietnamese grind glass up into little slivers, then slip them into the bottles. Then his voice boomed as he slapped me on the shoulder.

"That stuff will RIP your guts out, boy. Like takin' a belly wound. Don't buy NO gook shit! Got it, BOY!"

"Yea, man, thanks. I'm new in country, two days."

"Two days in 'Nam and you're a CORPORAL!"

"Came over late. I've been in for a year and a half."

"BOY, so have I, but I was a grunt out of boot camp and came right over HERE! I've been here thirteen months and I'm a private. Whatdya think of that, new boy?"

"Ashamed and scared."

"Well, well, I think you're gonna do JUST fine."

We passed through the marketplace in Cam-Lo Ville and I saw a plaster and brick type pagoda structure rising up, blank on all four sides. Like the people's stares. Then we passed some grave mounds. They were like little hills, the same size and rounded. I asked the black grunt about them and he said, "In 'Nam, boy, you'll find all the dead buried ABOVE ground." He brought his face close and peered intently into my eyes. "How do I look to you, boy?" "You look a little like Jimi Hendrix." "Boy, YOU and ME are gonna get along fine!"

Our convoy rumbled on. The older grunts in the truck turned and gave a heavy eyeball toward a ridge of hills passing on our right.

"What's that place?" I asked.

"Mudders Ridge! THEY OWN THAT!" The black grunt pointed his finger, cocked his thumb back and fired. "Third Marines kicked ASS on that ridge, boy!"

Camp Carroll sits on the peak of a high hill overlooking the vast expanse of valley on all four sides. It is the home of the 3rd Marine Regiment. They also have some big guns up here, 175s, and some tanks and 40-millimeter tracked vehicles. The Army mans the big guns. I traveled a winding road coming up.

There was a garbage dump, a big one for the whole camp, set into a large hole. At 4 p.m., the time our convoy arrived, they opened the wire gate and let the Vietnamese run in and grab as much garbage as they can. There must have been fifty Vietnamese crowding by the wire. Their clothes were torn and rotting. I waited for them to suddenly dissolve in front of me. When the gate opened I could see they were knocking each other down to get at the garbage.

Several marines were around them with rifles. They tried to keep order, but it was chaos. They shouted at the people like drill instructors. The people didn't listen, they just kept tearing at the garbage, stuffing their pockets. A marine shouted again, then fired a burst from his M-16 rifle, full-automatic. The rounds chewed up the ground by the feet of the Vietnamese. They didn't get excited or scared, or run. They stopped and stood silently waiting, expecting. There was no expression on their faces. I guess it's a nightly thing for them. The last few days at 4 p.m. I've heard rifle fire down by the dump. But they say nobody gets killed. It's a strange game.

Once inside the perimeter of the marine compound, it's a different world again. Inside the wire you feel more segregated and protected.

"This IS the world, boy," the wide-eyed black grunt said. "People ain't goin' home, they's just shippin' out to another foreign land, AGAIN!" He laughed, lifting one thigh and slapping his hand against it.

"Can you tell me your name, or am I still too new?"

"My name is PROUD, boy, that's it. You prove your shit HERE, boy, and you can be called anything you want."

Proud was shot through the cheeks of his ass during the Tet offensive of last year. He digs it. He told me he was on reactionary force with two platoons from Delta Company, when the Combined Actions Platoon in Cam-Lo came under heavy enemy small arms fire. He crawled out in the middle of the firing to save a badly wounded marine. He got shot, but still carried the guy back. Proud received the Bronze Star Medal for his heroism.

"Read this citation, BOY, I tell ya, I quote: 'was seriously wounded by intense small arms fire and, despite the pain of his wounds, maneuvered across the fire-swept terrain and saved the life of a wounded marine, carrying him across the exposed area to the safety of his comrades.' WOO-EEE, ya hear that, boy? That white man I saved was from my state. He didn't like NIGGERS!"

"Why'd you save him?"

"In combat you don't think about those things."

"This place is crazy, Proud."

"NO!" He brought his face real close to mine. "I'm sane, boy. You come to us crazy, do you understand? The 'Nam will make you so sane you'll sit and cry ALL THE TIME. Because you know. You'll see." Then he ran off.

On Tuesday I drew my weapon and equipment, but still was not assigned to a unit, so I waited. Proud was around a lot. He was a short-timer with only a week left. I was thinking I would be made a radio operator with Headquarters Company, 3rd Marines, and have a rear-area job. Proud, who had been in the bush his whole tour, seemed happy for me. Then the fist fell. The captain called me into his office on Wednesday and told me the news. 3rd Reconnaissance Battalion was taking heavy casualties and needed replacements, especially corporals and sergeants. I was to pack my gear, catch the next convoy, head back to Quang-Tri City with all my stuff, and report to them. I told Proud at lunch.

"Shit, boy, the ultimate fuck for you. Recon. You gonna see this country, them ridges. You gonna get REAL sane with recon." Proud lowered his head and looked at the floor. "You gonna be a bushman, boy. For thirteen months, if you make it. GODDAMN them, boy!"

"Hey, it's okay, Proud, you did your time, now I'm gonna do mine. You're going home. I'll be okay."

Proud was solemn for the first time since I'd met him.

"You're gonna get real sane." Then he walked briskly out of the hootch.

Proud came back to the hootch after supper. He was a hoop

player in high school and carried a basketball around, palming it in those big hands, or spinning it in perfect balance on the end of a fingertip. He sits next to me spinning the basketball.

"Hey, boy, you got to come to the show!"

"What show?"

"MY show, boy, MY SHOW! 1900 hours, other side of the mess hall. Be there, boy, BE THERE!" Then he was gone again.

At 1900 hours I walk behind the mess hall and there's Proud, with maybe fourteen grunts around him, and they seem to be making bets. Proud's limbering up, stretching his arms, cracking his knuckles, rubbing his fingers. He seemed happy as hell, grinning. There was a pile of money on the ground, looking like hundreds of dollars.

Then a marine tosses Proud a hand grenade, and the group walks away from him, retreating into fighting holes and bunkers. Proud stands in the middle by himself, fingering the hand grenade. He looks over at me.

"Get your ass DOWN, boy, I told you this was MY SHOW!" His eyes were wide and rolling. I jumped into a fighting hole with another grunt.

Proud took a deep breath, pulled the pin on the grenade, and let the spoon fly. He had about four seconds to do something with it. He began unscrewing it, unscrewing the top, the fuse, the device that exploded, from the body of the grenade. With deft hand, faster and faster, he spun the top of the grenade until it blurred.

He separated them just in time, throwing the body of the grenade one way, the fuse another. The fuse exploded harmlessly before it hit the ground. Proud let out his breath, then howled, his head thrown back like he was baying the moon. He bent over and slapped his thighs, then sauntered over to us.

The marines came out of the holes grumbling and cursing, handing wads of money to Proud. The guy in the hole with me says, "The son-of-a-bitch did it again."

"Again?"

"Yea, he's been doing this most of his tour. He's got an angel on his shoulder. Takes our money again and again." The grunt climbs out of the hole and walks over and pays Proud. I climb out and Proud comes and slaps me on the back.

"You like my show, boy?"

"You're gonna kill yourself, Proud."

"No, boy, you got it wrong, NEV-AH!" Then he leans by my ear and whispers, "I make the white man pay me to stay alive. You didn't see any black brothers bettin' against me, did you?"

"No, Proud."

"Be glad you're white, boy. Black is a tough war."

He raced off, wrapping his long arms around the shoulders of his patrons, walking them away, talking all the time to them.

"I think I'm slowing down. My hands are getting shakier. Look here, why, they're trembling. It was close that time, didn't you think it was CLOSE!"

"Yea, maybe," replied the grunt whose shoulder he was squeezing.

Proud told me later, "Them boys bought Proud a Cadillac! Can you IMAGINE, boy, a private in the Marine Corps driving a CADILLAC. I'm from Mississippi, Jackson. That place won't be the same, I tell ya, with me on the streets. I'm gonna blow 'em away! Proud's show is the BEST! Do you dig it, boy? Can you dig it? YOU GOT TO DIG IT!"

"You leave for the States tomorrow, Proud. You want to know my name before you leave?"

"No, boy, I don't want to know your name. I like you, but I'm afraid you're too soft for the bush. It's gonna kill the shit out of you. I don't want to hear your name 'cause I don't want to hear it again. I got too many names already. That's the sane, boy." Proud's eyes clouded with tears, but he choked them back. He reached out his paw of a hand and shook mine.

"Good luck to you, boy, stay SANE, WOO-EEE!"

He stood up, spun the basketball until it was balanced on the tip of a finger, and danced across the floor and out the door.

I never saw Proud again. We were both only starting on our long journeys home.

New Man

The truck convoy arriving from Camp Carroll stopped along the main road through the Quang-Tri Combat Base. Paul Timons jumped off one and looked around at the hundreds of weathered tents set in military rows.

The tents were made of thick, oily, olive-drab canvas that on both sides was supported from the inside. Lengths of rope reached out from around them, like many hands clenched tightly to the ground. The sinew-like muscles of the hemp strained to keep them from falling. They heaved in a dark heat that burned inside them, deep and thick, and stuck to you with the scent of damp rotting.

Paul stood by the side of the road and the convoy started again. It rumbled by, the truck beds packed with impassive faces. New men being delivered to the war.

Paul watched the last truck churn by in a barrel of dust, then turned and saw a marine, covered with sweat and dirt, standing on the other side of the road. Paul walked across to him. The marine smelled like the tents.

"Excuse me," Paul said, "could you tell me where 3rd Recon is?"

The marine looked at Paul's new jungle fatigues and smiled.

"You'll find 'em out there!" He jerked his head back and over his shoulder, toward the distant expanse of jungles and mountains. "You better git out there right away and find 'em!"

"I'll try, thanks," Paul said, turning to walk away.

"You're goin' the wrong way! Goddamn! Look, follow this road to that intersection there, see where I'm pointin'? Go to the right, and maybe three hundred meters up, you'll find what you're lookin' to get. Won't miss it!"

"Thanks."

"Nothing to it," the marine said, shrugging his shoulders.

Paul walked to the intersection, turned right, and looked again at the marine standing in the road. The marine saw Paul looking, grinned broadly, and, with a great sweep of his arm, swung around and pointed again over his shoulder. Then the marine turned away and walked on.

Paul found the battalion. A big red sign was planted in the ground. It said: "3rd Reconnaissance Battalion, 3rd Marine Division, Fleet Marine Force, Pacific." And across the top, the words "Swift, Silent, Deadly."

Paul walked into the area and found a smaller red sign poked in the ground outside a tent. It said: "Headquarters Co."

He walked in accompanied by the rattling clatter of typewriters set up on makeshift desks. A stocky sergeant approached him. He was clean-shaven but soaked in sweat.

"Can I help you, Corporal?" the sergeant said, looking Paul up and down.

"Yea, Sarge, I'm reporting to you from 3rd Marines, up at Carroll."

"New man, eh?" the sergeant said, smiling.

"Six days," Paul replied.

"Only 390 days left and a wake-up. Gimme your service record book and have a seat." The sergeant motioned for Paul to sit in one of the canvas chairs.

As soon as Paul settled in the canvas chair, it folded in on him like the jaws of a trap, and he crumpled to the floor. Everyone in the tent erupted in laughter.

"Give the new man a Purple Heart! Six days and he's already tripped a booby-trap!"

Paul stood up, angry and embarrassed, and brushed himself off.

"You're goin' to Alpha Company. Welcome to 'Nam!" the sergeant said, laughing.

Baptism of Fire

Ellison Ivery was an M-79 grenade-launcher marine attached to a recon team in the Second Platoon. He was a big proud black man from Durham, North Carolina. He knew racism and alienation and beatings from whites long before he began the deep, long-range reconnaissance patrols in enemy-infested areas for the defense of his nation, a country that had oppressed him and his people for all the generations he could ever recall. It was a great weight and hung, with his anger, like a dark cross from his powerful neck. He did not like white people. So he stayed with the other blacks, mostly the militants, who had taken lately to wearing black gloves all the time and special handshaking each other, and holding secret meetings where they reveled in their hatred of white oppression. Ellison let out his anger at these meetings. Always at the end he would raise a heavily muscled right arm, the sinews twisted, and smash his huge fist on the table. In silence, the others would listen. The rest of the time Ellison kept completely to himself, did his job, ran patrol after patrol, until the months of horror and war and combat drifted toward him and swept past. He had ceased long ago to believe in God. He had ceased to believe in anything.

Finally, after the many months of hidden alienation and homelessness set themselves on him day and night, he was a short-timer. Two weeks left. One more patrol. A replacement was coming. All he had to do was train the new guy. Then he could go home.

Ellison was coming off his thirty-fourth patrol and was very tired. He felt the familiar descent of the chopper, the engines whining, then screaming, as the skids settled down on the soft landing strip by the battalion headquarters at Quang-Tri. He jumped off, all wet and mud- and gear-soaked from the humidity of the jungle, and walked tired-legged across the little grassy airstrip. He looked at the replacement. The man's skin was as white as a newborn baby's.

The replacement held out his hand to the black man. The proud black bushman looked down at him and said, "We got nothin' to shake about."

"My name's Paul Timons," the marine replied. "They said you'd train me before you go home. I'm happy you're going home."

"Don't be happy for me, asshole!" Ellison roared. His eyes took on the look of a storm. Paul still had his hand out. Slowly, he lowered it.

"I'm sorry," Paul said.

At that moment Ellison caught sight of a large crucifix Paul wore. It was bright silver and the figure of the suffering Christ nailed upon it was unmistakable in its facial features of pain. Ellison could even see the nails struck in at the hands and feet, and the spear wound in his side. A great pity welled up inside Ellison, something he had not felt for a long time. He reached out and engulfed the white hand with his, and said, "Welcome to 'Nam, brother."

In the next week Ellison did everything he could for Paul. He got him settled with the team, found him a cot and a footlocker, took him to the mess hall, showed him around the company area, and drilled Paul on the dangers of jungle warfare. Paul listened intently to everything Ellison told him. All this was done around a constant flow of information regarding his M-79. The small shotgun-like grenade launcher fired a single squat shell that was lobbed rather than propelled like a rifle. Ellison took Paul to a range where they fired over a hundred rounds, and Paul was good.

After a week, the team got orders for patrol. This would be Paul's baptism of fire and Ellison felt scared for him.

Paul prayed a lot, clutching his big crucifix. Ellison felt a great feeling for Paul and the beginnings of the pangs of brotherly love. And Ellison felt scared and tried to push the feeling away. Yet, for Paul, Ellison could do no wrong. Paul looked upon him as an idol.

The night before the patrol the wind picked up until it was swirling the dust in spirals up the company street. The inner flaps of the tent, in which the men prepared themselves, were ruffling and cracking like a whip. Ellison helped Paul pack his rucksack properly, then showed him how to prepare his weapon and carry extra rounds.

When they were done they walked outside.

"Paul," Ellison began. It was the first time he had used Paul's name. "Stick by me and listen to me. If we hit the shit I want you close. Do you understand?"

"I understand, Ellison."

"How old are you, Paul?"

"I'm eighteen. How old are you?"

"I just turned nineteen," Ellison said.

"You don't believe in God, do you, Ellison?"

"No, I don't believe in anything. There is nothing."

"There is a God who loves us, Ellison."

"Ain't no God who ever loved me, Paul. He's hunted me all my life."

"I don't think God hunts people. He loves. He cares. He's taking you home."

"Yes," Ellison said. "But, Paul, there's one thing you gotta learn. There is no God in war."

"I'll say a prayer for you tonight," Paul replied.

"Okay, Paul, I'll say a prayer too. It'll be the first one in a long time."

The wind had picked up and Ellison didn't like it. It had risen from a swish and had become a shriek that dragged loose boxes and cans and rolled them down the company street. Paul squeezed Ellison's hand and went inside. Soon Ellison heard Paul praying.

Ellison looked up into the dark night. He tried to look so deep his gaze would pass the galaxies and stars and rush headlong toward the threshold of the heavens. He lowered his head and pressed his hands together. He closed his eyes. He wanted to believe just once.

"God. If you're there. Take care of Paul. Watch over him. And please. Take me home."

The night flew and early daylight found the team separated in two helicopters flying in circles eight klicks northeast of the Rock-pile. There was a high jungle ridge where they were to be inserted. Ellison and Paul were in the second chopper going in. Now the first chopper, with the first four men of the eight-man team aboard, circled once and began its descent. Ellison and Paul watched intently from the second helicopter. The first craft descended. Down, down it went until it hovered over the landing zone. Suddenly there was an explosion and the aircraft settled and disintegrated on the hill. The second chopper, its engines screaming, descended quickly. The door gunners rattled off rounds from their machine guns and they began to go in. Ellison roared over the machine guns and screaming of the chopper's engines.

"This is gonna be bad! Stay close to me!"

As they descended into the landing zone next to the burning aircraft Ellison could hear the "pop-pop-pop" of a North Vietnamese .51-caliber machine gun. He knew that's what got the others. Not a booby-trap. The chopper went in fast, the door-gunners blasting from both machine guns, and didn't even touch down. The four men jumped from the aircraft, weapons blazing.

The helicopter immediately gained altitude, turning away and banking hard to escape the enemy anti-aircraft fire.

Ellison shoved Paul behind a downed tree and told him to lob rounds down the rise, where the fire was coming from. Paul responded instantly. He placed round after round in, and pumped them over the rise in the direction of the firing. Rounds poured in on the four of them. Tree branches were severed by the enemy bullets and fell on them where they lay firing. Enemy ammunition impacted on the dead tree Paul lay behind. Yet, again and again he raised his head, sighted in, and fired. Paul was relentless.

Ellison made his way carefully to the burning chopper. The stench of burned flesh filled his senses and he felt he would vomit. The aircraft was glowing with intense heat, a burnt frame with charred seated bodies, others lying flat and slumped over. Skillfully Ellison made his way back to the other three. All four poured suppressing fire down into the valley.

They were shooting down the south side of the slope but hadn't seen a single enemy soldier. The team's radio operator, his headset pressed to his ear, reported that an emergency helicopter had been dispatched and would try to get them out. It would be coming within minutes.

When the rescue helicopter arrived on the scene, the pilot decided to try to hover on the north side of the slope, away from the firing, so the team could race aboard. It was a big, CH-46 transport, capable of carrying up to twenty marines. The wind was coming in quick gusts. The pilot had hovered the craft like a big bird in a fierce wind. He backed the tail, with its loading ramp, to the side of the hill and tried to steady the bird. Hard as the pilot fought to control it, the chopper swayed left and right, and the nose lifted and fell.

Ellison screamed for the first two men to run and board. They cautiously made their way across the rise, down the north side and scrambled inside the craft. Now just the two M-79 men were left lobbing rounds. Ellison and Paul fought side by side. They were brothers forever.

"You go now, Paul!" Ellison roared.

Paul lobbed one more round out and ran up over the ridge and down the little rise into the safety of the bird. The pilot struggled to hover. Ellison came running. The chopper lurched in a big gust of wind, the nose came up and the back rotor blade came down. As Ellison ran to board the helicopter, the back rotor blade was too low. It struck him with the force of a grenade going off, disintegrating his head in a spray of blood, bone fragments, and brain tissue.

Ellison still walked up the ramp. Paul stared. Ellison's legs were like a one-year-old's, and he began collapsing. He took one more hesitant step toward Paul, then fell heavily to his knees and toppled over into Paul's lap.

Paul caught Ellison's body under the armpits, wrapped his arms around him and pulled him close. From Ellison's throat dark blood surged like a boiling stew, soaking Paul. Paul began crying with deep sobs as he looked down. His tears were immediately absorbed in the wound.

Paul held Ellison close all the way back to Bravo Med at Quang-Tri where the casualties were brought. The corpsmen there had to pry Ellison's body from Paul's grip.

In a daze, Paul shuffled behind them like an old man. The corpsmen carried Ellison's body and placed it on a gurney outside the Med. They went inside to get a body bag.

Paul looked down at the headless torso. He wanted Ellison to come back, to somehow teach him more. He waited. In his head he heard Ellison's voice, his strong voice, saying: "Your Baptism of Fire, you're welcomed into the Church of War. There are no gods.

There are no scriptures to live by. You suffer them as you go along. And you must enter. In war you cannot get up from where you are kneeling, at the altar of your death, and run out while the bells are ringing. Paul, you'll have to listen to the song, long and long. Only horror has the faith here."

Paul took the big crucifix from his neck and laid it on Ellison's chest. The cross was covered with blood that had blackened on the silver.

The night was beginning to settle in, and from all its immortal silence no answers came. Paul walked away, alone.

HUNGERS

For thirty-seven days, eighteen marines, in their fighting position on a barren outpost atop a hill in the Balong Valley, suffered the pounding monsoon rains.

The hill was code-named "November" and was a radio relay for the main headquarters in Quang-Tri that was home for the battalion. They transferred the calls into the bush where recon marines were operating and were the constant twenty-four hour vigilance for the teams that hunkered down and endured the daily regimen of their patrols.

The hill jutted up like a knuckle on your fist and, like your knuckled fist, fell off to three sides in deep slides, except for the west, which extended up the arm connecting the jungle's body. The enemy grew from there. Over bent, sloping shoulders, across arched, muscular backs, tensed with sinewed muscles of hills and ridges, down short, powerful legs that extended east to the South China Sea.

The hill was mud, thick and ankle-deep, and marines slipped as they moved about, fortifying their fighting positions with sandbags. Others, working around the perimeter, strung concertina wire in ever-building piles and rows.

The fog and rain had held steady for the last twenty-seven days. Re-supply helicopters were grounded. The marines were starving. Each man ate only one can of C-rations a day.

Through the long days of rain and filling sandbags and digging bunkers, and the long nights of watches, their rifles pointing down into the darkness of the wire, their eyes straining down barrels, they did not complain. Days passed quietly, uneventfully. Nights contained all the sounds, everything.

Something always seemed to be moving through the corners of

Paul Timons' vision. North Vietnamese soldiers slipping through the wire. He thought he could hear them breathing, only ten meters from his position, turning his claymore mines around so the blast would hit him. Then, slithering back out, smiles on their snake-like lips, they'd tie a string to the concertina wire and lead it back toward the body of the jungle. They'd pull the string and rattle the wire, hoping he'd blow the claymores. Or one of them would make a mistake coming through or going out and get caught in the razor-sharp barbs of the wire.

The goddamn wire was rattling! Paul thought of throwing a grenade. Grenades never give away your position. Paul pulled the pin on one, holding the spoon down.

It could be a rock ape or rats, he thought. The empty C-ration cans, hanging on the wire with pebbles in them, rattled again. Shit! Paul's hand cramped. He quickly switched the grenade carefully to his other. Shit! It was quiet. It was quiet for ten minutes. Paul tried to stick the pin back in. He couldn't.

"Hey, Jerry, bro, I got a question." Paul squatted in the sandbagged fighting hole and whispered through a shelter-half directly behind him. The shelter-half covered the front of a small, carved-out mud cave, with piles of sandbags against the sides and in layers on top. Jerry squinted at Paul where he lay miserable on the damp floor.

"I'm here," Jerry replied, yawning.

"I thought I heard gooks in the wire, ya know? And I pulled the pin on a grenade. And then it got quiet. And I can't get the goddamn pin back in." Paul thrust his arm in at Jerry, holding the live frag in his right fist.

"Well, son, my best advice would be to throw the motherfucker." Jerry lay back down and closed his eyes.

Paul pulled his head out from under the shelter-half and stood again in the steady, pounding rain. He looked at the frag, shrugged his shoulders, then threw it down into the wire and ducked his head. BLAM!

Paul stayed crouched in the hole, the rain beating on his helmet with tiny explosions. He stood up and listened to the thousands of impacts, shivering until dawn.

On the morning of the thirty-eighth day, Paul, a corporal and the man presently in charge on this small hill, walked up to the communications bunker. He ducked down inside, his poncho glistening wet, and sat wearily next to Jack Edwards, a friend from his native New York State. Paul lit a Lucky Strike cigarette, left over from World War II, from a pack of four that came in every box of C-rations. The boxes in the last drop of Cs they got were stamped 1943 and 1944. Well, Paul thought, at least it's getting close to the end of the war.

"Well, Jack, what da ya think of this shit?"

Jack turned away from the radio he was monitoring and looked with sympathetic eyes at Paul.

"It sucks and I'm getting hungry. I can handle not takin' a shower or washin' for a month. I don't mind not gettin' laid. But chow, man, ya know?"

"Yea, well, I got an idea." Paul pulled his head closer. He motioned with his hand for Jack to bend his ear toward him. He whispered, "I'm gonna call battalion. But I'm gonna promote myself first. I can't jerk no chains. So I decided to promote myself, and see if it'll pull enough weight to get us some chow. Dig?"

"Yea, Paul, but your ass is grass and they're lawnmowers."

"Fuck it. I'm hungry."

"What are you promoting yourself to?"

"Well, first I thought I'd be a second or first lieutenant. Then I decided a major would be perfect. No more Echo four Tango. I'm Oscar four Tango now."

Jack saluted Paul and gave him the handset to the radio. Jack was grinning. Paul lifted the handset and keyed it.

"Grainy Sand, Grainy Sand, November, over."

"November, this is Grainy Sand, go."

"Roger, Grainy Sand, this is Oscar four Tango, I repeat, Oscar four Tango. And I have been here for some time and my men are hungry! Do you copy, Grainy Sand? I want a re-supply run for my men. Do you understand? Over."

"November, this is Grainy Sand. I copy. Oscar four Tango requests emergency re-supply. Over."

"Grainy Sand, November. You have a solid. How long before?

Over."

"We'll get right back to you, November."

Paul gave the handset back to Jack.

"Get out the good silverware, Jack. We're gonna eat!"

"They might hang your ass, Paul."

"Naw, they're gonna feed us." Paul opened the shelter-half to the sound of the persistent rain. "Let me know soon as they call."

The deep fog held thickest at night and through the morning. By mid-afternoon some would burn off, but it stayed rainy and cold.

The next morning Paul visited with Eagle Stanley, an American Indian who joined the Corps to be a warrior. His father had been chief of their tribe. Paul liked to sit with Eagle early, over first coffee. The sun rose as if it were rising out of the sea and, on the few clear days, provided the only enjoyable moment they shared. Dawn was the time the jungle lay for its short rest. After dawn battles started, before dawn battles broke off. It was one of those peculiar events that marks a war in its individual way. Eagle had a manner of speaking that took Paul away from Vietnam. Sipping his coffee quietly next to Eagle, usually he would simply listen, having only to look at the Indian to make him speak.

"Paul, I look beyond the clouds and sea. I am more bird this morning than I have ever been. I'm sitting here thinking I could fly off this hill, over that valley, and not stop until I reach home." Eagle sipped his coffee. "If you want to go with me, Paul, just look out there." Eagle pointed. "And imagine yourself free in the clouds. Not a bad breakfast to ease the hunger pangs, eh?"

"Yeh, bro, fills me up fine."

Jack ran out of the communications bunker and shouted for Paul. Paul moved quickly to him, slipping in the running mud.

"What's up?"

"I got Seaworthy 5 on the air, a chopper man! And he says he's got a re-supply drop for us!"

"Tell Jerry to get some pop-up flares, and a few men down to the landing zone. I'll get the portable radio ready and start this guy down." Jack ran off.

Paul went in the bunker, sat down, and casually crossed his legs. He picked up the handset and keyed it.

"Seaworthy 5, this is November, over."

Paul lit a cigarette. The sound of a strained voice, talking over the roar of sweeping rotor blades, rose in his ear.

"November, Seaworthy 5. We have a re-supply drop coming in on you. Over."

"Roger, Seaworthy. I suggest hover toward LZ and we will fire flares straight up from center of LZ. You spot them, hover down. I'll direct. Over."

"Roger, November. Comin' at you low as I can. Any strong winds down there or enemy fire lately?"

"Negative, Seaworthy, peaceful. Over."

"Here we come, November."

Paul dropped the handset, snuffed out the cigarette, turned and grabbed the portable radio. He slung it on his back and keyed the handset to test it, heard the crackle on the other radio, and ran out of the bunker and down to the landing zone.

"Middle of LZ, Jerry!" Paul shouted. "Ding some pop-ups straight up. We got food comin'!"

Jerry ran to the middle, while other marines lay in a circle around him, their rifles covering the jungle. Jerry pulled the caps off and jammed the bottom of a pop-up and it took off, a small star cluster racing through the fog and rain. He did another. Paul listened to the chopper's sound coming closer while he paid attention to the radio handset.

"November, Seaworthy 5. Got the pop-ups. Will hover over. Then start down. We're all yours. Over."

"Roger, Seaworthy, you're in safe hands."

Paul heard the chopper through the mist move directly over them, then begin to come down. Closer and closer it came until turbulence began to whisp the fog.

"Seaworthy, November. You sound good. Right on. No visual contact yet."

"Roger, November," the calm voice replied.

"Got ya, Seaworthy! You're dead center of LZ."

"Roger, November, we have visual contact also. You guys hungry?"

"We're starving!"

"Roger that, November. We've been delivering all over. Making people happy today."

As the chopper came in to settle, the pilot turned and smiled at Paul, giving him a thumbs-up salute. Paul returned it. Then Paul saw the pilot push his microphone closer to his lips.

"Merry Christmas, November! Merry Christmas!"

That's right, Paul thought. The next day would be Christmas day, 1968.

"Merry Christmas, Seaworthy. Thanks. Over."

The chopper's back ramp lowered and crew members began throwing large boxes out. The ramp closed and the chopper gained power.

The chopper's rear wheels were tangled in the concertina wire surrounding the small landing zone. As the craft lifted up, two large coils of concertina wire hung down. The chopper turned suddenly and swept low across the landing zone, the pilot and co-pilot smiling and waving.

"Get the fuck down!" "Lay flat!" "That dirty motherfucker!"

Marines screamed and dove for cover.

Paul saw three men caught by the wire, dragging and whipping across the ground. Two were deeply slashed and flung off to the side. But the third was hooked around the throat, dragged a few feet bouncing, his hands frantically clawing at the wire, then shot from the earth, jerked high out over the valley. Paul watched him hanging limp like dead prey in a bird's talons.

"Seaworthy, November! You caught wire! You caught a man!"

"What? What?" came the staticed reply.

The sound of the helicopter became more distant, blending into the deep consuming clouds that rolled and bulged like pregnant women and spread like a dark secret raining upon the land.

Paul immediately radioed battalion for them to notify the helicopter of the cargo they carried. Paul unstrapped the radio from his back, angrily threw it on the ground and kicked it. Their corpsman, Doc Heinz, was bending over the two wounded, wrapping bandages and tying tourniquets.

"Who'd he get?" Paul screamed.

"He got Eagle," Jerry replied solemnly.

Doc Heinz stopped the bleeding and requested a medevac. Paul radioed battalion for them to send one, and he was asked how serious the wounds were. Paul wanted to empty a magazine into the radio. The wounds weren't that serious, they just bled a lot. Permission for the day was denied. Maybe tomorrow.

No one touched the boxes of food. They sat together in silence on top of the hill staring through the rain in the direction the chopper had gone.

Paul knew there was nothing that could take him away from Vietnam, nothing to quench his thirsts or ease his hungers.

"Hell, man," Jerry said, "nothin' we can do about Eagle now, nothin' we can do about shit up here! So why should we starve? The least we can do for Eagle is chow down, have a big party for him!"

Jack jumped up and shouted, "Let's go, men! Let's eat!" The marines yelled and ran down to the landing zone and hauled the boxes up the hill to the top. They threw them down and Paul ceremoniously cut open the first box with a bayonet. Inside were six large cans of sauerkraut.

"What the fuck, over. What the fuck, over," Paul said.

"What kind of shit they pulling here?" Jerry said with disbelief.

"They're all just fuckin' sauerkraut!" Ross, a machinegunner, said.

"They threw us off the wrong shit. This shoulda gone to a damn mess hall in Dong-Ha or Quang-Tri. All that fuckin' trouble. Goddamn." Paul turned away.

"Fuck 'em! Let's eat!" Jerry said.

They all began laughing, tearing hysterically at the boxes, opening cans, and all over the hill small fires were built and sauerkraut was cooked eighteen different ways. They ate the sauerkraut until their stomachs bulged.

"Aw, fuck," Paul said, holding his stomach with both hands.

"Aw, fuck," Jerry said.

Christmas eve came on fast and darkness again abided in all things. The night lay still. The marines hunched into their weapons. The Christmas truce was on and the marines were wary. They stayed on full alert. No unnecessary conversation. Everyone up and ready to fight.

Paul's heart froze. He heard a long moan from one corner of the hill, a moan that congealed his heart and stopped his breath. His eyes widened as he listened. The moan rose again, higher pitched. Then Paul heard it. A long, stiff fart cracked the night. From another part of the hill another marine moaned, then another deep fart. Paul felt his guts churning. Gas was building and it hurt.

"Merry Christmas!" Paul screamed as he cut a terrific fart. The marines applauded. "Get some!" one marine said. Paul started singing "Silent Night" and by the second line all the marines joined in.

Outside the wire, just inside the rim of trees surrounding the perimeter, a squad of North Vietnamese soldiers squatted in silence. They were planning a Christmas eve attack. The NVA looked at each other, the squad leader cocking his head to one side in deep thought. The twelve NVA were nervous about the noise. They were as superstitious about the Americans' Christmas as they were about their own Tet New Year.

The NVA soldier in charge laughed quietly.

"Marines crazy tonight. This is not a good time to attack these marines." He led and the others followed. They moved away from the singing, down into the valley. Far enough distant, they shouldered their weapons and smiled.

"Marines dinky-dou. Very crazy." The leader spun his finger around his head to emphasize his point.

"Jerry! I think I hear something out there!" Paul said. "Be quiet!"

"Fuck 'em, Paul, let 'em come join our party." Jerry leaned into his M-60 machine gun, sweeping the barrel through the darkness, and kept singing.

They all sang together.

"Silent night, holy night, all is calm, all is bright..."

A Letter Home

January 13, 1969
Quang-Tri, Vietnam

Hello Friend,

Just a short note to let you know I'm okay. I've run eight patrols now (starting to get salty, I guess). The first one was the worst, I lost a good friend. We really flew into the shit. I really don't know how to explain it. Or the others.

I started off an M-79 grenade launcher man, switched to secondary pointman on my fourth patrol, then became pointman. I guess I did it to prove to my buddies I wasn't afraid to walk there. Try to set an example. I still want to believe we can win.

I'm scared as hell, very, very scared. And now I sense a deeper fear, that we've lost. I'm becoming more sure of it, so at times I want to give up.

Since Johnson halted the bombing of the north this past October we've been pounded on a regular basis. A shit load of incoming. And now they have free reign to throw anything at us they want. They hit us with 130 mm and 152 mm artillery (they're real accurate with this stuff) and 122 mm rockets. They hit us during breakfast, lunch, and dinner (it's always their choice). They hit us about the time we go to sleep, or just after we go to sleep. They hit us when they know our minds do not want to be on this. They mix it up so we're real edgy all the time. I think they're starting to have a grand time with the war.

They think they're winning and those of us on the line are beginning to think they're right. I'm beginning to wonder what we could possibly mean by "victory." How do we win? Now? I haven't got any idea except we're supposed to fight to the death. Death has the clearest meaning here.

I've seen fourteen marines killed since I've been here, and not *one* dead NVA. What the hell is going on?

I must try to hold on to a thin thread of hope we can still win it. I must do this or go crazy. Some of the guys have already conceded we've lost, and they, too, are lost. They can't fight anymore because they've lost their will, and will is the only thing that keeps us moving forward now.

Once any of us concedes, gives it up, we become sort of living death. We look like bodies that don't have enough sense to lie down and be zippered shut. It's the disease we all dread. I *must* keep my will, I must *believe*. If only in myself, I must...listen, I hear the distant sound of guns...gotta run...know how much you're loved!

Paul

A Letter Home

March 14, 1969
Quang-Tri, Vietnam

Hello Friend,

Thanks so much for your last letter. It brings me my only hope when I know people like you care, truly care, for what we're going through.

I agree with you about the war. Tet is over and we stopped them, (or them us) whatever it is this thing is measured with. I got my first Purple Hurt Medal, but nothing to worry about, just a small piece of shrapnel in my left knee. I would like to tell you about Christmas and New Years and this whole Tet affair, but I don't want to waste words and, besides, the night is drawn solid as rock and the day flows out of wounds and I'm kinda, well, somewheres.

You mentioned in your letter that the war is lost. Yes, of course! What are we doing? Don't ask me!

I'm trying to figure out how I can continue. I've been here five months and have eight months left! My body is not transmitting properly, need to change the battery, or frequency, need a bigger antenna! We fought some pretty hard battles during the month of February. I killed a bunch of gooks. Shit! Do you copy?

I'm trying to concentrate on this war, trying to do my best. But my best isn't good enough, all of our "bests" aren't good enough! Which is the way, I mean, how do I, or what is, home?

Jesus, my friend, this jungle can swallow you whole! Implant your ass right in the ole turf! I'm unraveling like a ball of twine. When I get to the end there's nothing there, nothing!

We all know the war is lost, I know it, the guy next to me knows it. Why the fuck don't they pull us out of here? Okay, we *all* know it, right? What's this continuing? Arlington's not full yet? There's an undug hole in the veteran's plot of our cemetery that has a sign staked in it. Says "Reserved."

The draft dodgers and war resisters only got into this thing when the draft opened up. Where the hell were they prior to losing their exemptions? We get letters all the time from these people. Never got 'em before. Now they're all hot for trots to end it, now their asses are hangin' in the wind. Now their swingin' dicks might get caught fuckin' the country and they'll have to, well, fight! Yea, bring 'em on over. God forbid their Friday night concerts and beer parties and horny toads might have to plunge the ole dipstick into something thicker!

Yea, I'm carrying on! Racing! It's just, my friend, I'm sorry. I don't know what's happening to me, I feel like blowing up all the time, just, you know, WHAM!

I walk around like I've swallowed a hand grenade. At the slightest provocation I spit out the pin and feel the spoon fly!

Tick...tick...tick...Do you know how much time is contained in three seconds? I never gave it any thought before, but now I'm so aware of it! Eternities! Lifetimes! Generations! Tick...tick...tick...Histories! Economies! Mathematics! Tick...tick...tick...Religions! Philosophies! Medicine! All gone, all puffed to dust, in between, squeezed out to the last drop! One lousy second holds all of life in me now! Holds it in, and is ready to let it go! Ah...woof...blam...that's Paul smeared across the ground. Never thought his guts looked like that! What a weird shape, his heart? Brains are strange...I've seen 'em a few times, in chunks...tick...tick...tick...Goodbye!

Paul

Billy Sunday

Billy Sunday was home on point. When his recon team drew patrols in the Northern I Corps, Billy Sunday led them, he walked first. It was his calling and it was his home. He had become like a keen animal, his nose catching every scent, the dampness of old campfires burned out, the smell of unwashed bodies, the slight opening of a spider-trap. His nostrils would flare as he felt it out. Every nerve-end in his body became electrified, snarling and snapping. Primordial bolts of energy pulsed and throbbed in his grip.

He was deadly with his rifle. At the snap of a bolt, a pin pulled, any metallic sound, a whisper passed in the wind, up his spine would go the bolts of electricity, exploding in his brain, racing madly through his arms that clutched the weapon of man's fate. The weapon would rise to his shoulder and just as quickly, static power bursting in his brain, he would sight in and fire. Fear raged on the edge he walked on, the weapon exploding and kicking against him with a recoil that held the power of death. He killed when and where he could. In war he was considered a hero for that.

Now in April of 1969 he rose early in the morning deep in the jungle south of Khe Sanh. He loved to watch the beautiful sunrises and just before, if the sky was clear, the dark night would be an incredible display of galaxies and stars. Never had he existed in an air as pure as this. The stars would light up the canvas of darkness and cast a pale haze that, as it descended earthward, would become fog growing in ghostly wisps that, in silent drifting, shrouded the valley below the rise the team was on.

As the bright sun broke the horizon rock apes high in the upper branches of the trees in the triple canopy jungle would begin whooping and whooping like roosters ka-doing the dawn. Billy Sunday smiled. He was just as much an animal as they were. He belonged there.

While he watched the sunrise Billy thought of how he had

ended up on this patrol. The higher-ups back at basecamp had sent him to interrogators' school down in DaNang. For thirty days he could have had easy duty.

He had just come off a patrol in the Ashau Valley when they told him. He had been taking part in a battalion-size operation in the far southern corner of the Khe Sanh Valley by the border of the Ashau. He wanted to be in the bush. He wanted to kill. He thought of the twelve confirmed kills he already had. The rock apes whooped and Sunday smiled. Then he thought deeper.

When the helicopter touched down at DaNang carrying him to the thirty-day school where they would teach him to speak Vietnamese, Sunday was angry. It was pointless, he took no prisoners. That was his first rule of the bush. Waste them.

He walked into the terminal building and got directions to the school's compound. It was within walking distance. Billy felt lost as he made his way through the crowded streets. People were shoving and shouting and running everywhere. Trucks coughed and choked and puffed along, throwing out smelly exhaust fumes. Hundreds of bicycles weaved around him and everywhere among the masses was a sense of urgent flight.

The people wore clean civilian clothes. They carried no weapons. Sunday was a bushman and everyone he passed in DaNang knew that.

He wore boots that were white and broken in cracks across the tops. His clothes were faded and torn and dried mud was caked on them. He carried a rucksack with his few belongings and on his shoulder straps hung several grenades. He draped his rifle gently in his arms, a magazine of ammo in, locked and loaded. Across his shoulders, criss-crossed, were two bandoliers holding pouches for his rifle's magazines. Hung over his neck and hanging down was a grease gun, a World War II weapon that fired bursts from a clip of .45 caliber ammunition. Big and powerful for close-in fighting. On Sunday's web belt were canteens, a machete, and a pouch holding six more clips for the grease gun.

Sunday's face was streaked with camouflage greasepaint running in straight rivulets down his cheeks, mixing with the sweat that soaked his whole body as he walked down the hot, sticky streets. The people stopped and stared. They said nothing to him. They cautiously moved out of his way.

He walked to the headquarters of the school, shuffling along in his bush pride. He was a jungle animal. His worn and weatherbeaten bush cover felt good on his head. By the time he entered the air-conditioned office of the school he had made up his mind. He strode up to the officer in charge, who was drinking a cold beer, and told him he wanted to go back to his outfit, that he didn't want to be there. He wanted to go back where he belonged.

The young officer in his freshly pressed uniform thought Sunday was crazy. Too much combat, he thought. He tried to reason with Billy. He tried to tell him about the hot meals three times a day, the air-conditioning, the movies every night, the hot showers and clean sheets, the whores, the beer, the beach for swimming with the beautiful sea and swaying trees. Why, men had begged on their knees for this assignment, the young officer said.

Sunday looked around, his eyes squinting hard in the cold breeze from the air-conditioning.

"You just don't goddamn understand!" Sunday said, his nostrils flaring. Then he turned and walked out.

In a day he made his way back up north to his outfit. The brass were mad and told him if he wanted the bush that's where they'd keep him, and they sent him out on this patrol.

Now the sun was full above the jungle of the Khe Sanh Valley. The fog had lifted and Sunday felt the warmth and smiled. The patrol was beginning to stir and soon they would be moving out.

Billy picked up the binoculars by his rucksack, took off the protective lens caps and focused on the valley below. As he searched the hidden recesses of the jungle for any movement, he caught sight of a large tiger framed in the dawning light.

The tiger had struck and wounded a rock ape that had strayed to the ground to scavenge for food. Sunday could see the monkey was bleeding. It dove into some thick brush trying to escape, but appeared too weak to climb.

The tiger snarled, then on muscular haunches, pounced into the brush. The leaves and branches shuddered like a last breath, and the conquering silence of the jungle settled in.

Sunday could not see the tiger anymore. It had stealthily disappeared into the shadows. He lowered the binoculars and smiled. Soon the patrol would be moving out.

After a C-ration breakfast eaten in silence, except for a few low whispers and hand signals, the patrol packed up and moved out. Sunday led them off the rise, down into the valley. With the sun ascending higher, everything was broken by shafts of bright lights intertwined with shadows moving. The wind through the branches in trees, the sun's rays slanted.

They had walked for four hours when Billy suddenly stumbled onto a small trail used by North Vietnamese soldiers. It was about a foot wide and Sunday could tell by the deep, worn rut that it was well used. He motioned with his hand for the rest of the patrol to get down. Immediately and silently they slipped left and right, blending into the jungle.

Sunday looked to his right, turned, took one step, then froze. His nostrils flared. Thirty meters from him a North Vietnamese soldier appeared. The soldier had his eyes down, concentrating on the trail. Sunday snapped his rifle to his shoulder and squeezed the trigger. A clatter of whams echoed through the valley.

Clutching his stomach with one hand and his chest with the other, the NVA soldier fell back into some thick brush.

Sunday jumped to one side of the trail and squatted. He was thinking of the tiger. A smile came to his face. He snarled.

Corporal Higgans, who had been walking behind Billy, crawled up to him, his rifle cradled in his arms.

"Only one?"

"Yeah," Sunday replied.

"You waste him?" Higgans asked, looking down the trail.

"Yeah, I got the fucker."

"Let's check 'em out."

Higgans crawled back to the rest of the patrol and Sunday heard the quiet crackling of radio transmissions. Then Billy waved his hand and they moved out.

They stayed off the trail about three meters in the brush and moved parallel to it, slowly advancing to where the enemy soldier had fallen. Sunday felt like the tiger. As he moved closer, his heart pounded with the ferocity of the hunt.

Billy saw blood on the trail and blood splattered on leaves by some brush beside it. Sunday cautiously approached, his rifle braced into his shoulder, his eyes straining down the sights.

"I am a tiger!" Sunday said.

He stepped out on the trail, his eyes all the time focused on the bloody brush. Billy never saw the thin wire strung across the trail.

The booby-trap exploded and the conquering silence of the jungle settled in.

Education of a Pointman

The six-man recon team walked single file across the sun-baked earth pock-marked with craters, then moved across the brown barren ground that was a viscous memory heavy and hot, a hardness that burned down on them in waves which reflected off the cracked earth a silence thick and dead.

They walked past the last bunkers surrounding the Con Thien outpost and moved toward the wire. The high sun and humidity had them soaked in sweat and a slight wind made their clothes stick to their bodies.

Paul walked point. He carefully separated the strands of concertina wire. Once through the wire, he adjusted the strap of his rifle across his shoulder. As he broke through into tall elephant grass and stepped down into a small gully, he pressed hard into the front of the weapon, bearing down into its weight, into the stuttering death that would fly from its barrel. The rifle alone seemed to pull him through.

The other five men followed but stayed far enough behind the pointman that Paul always felt alone. When he turned once to look, he could no longer see the Con Thien outpost, he could hardly see the second man in the team struggling forward. Around them the jungle closed in and tightened its grip, in the tense snapping of branches being broken and brushed aside, in the sharp cracking of grass and sticks being broken underfoot.

Paul opened a Lensamatic compass hanging around his neck, held it out and watched the needle settle. He turned, then stepped out faster, picking up the pace, fiercer, all his life surging forward in the rhythmic pounding of his heart. The end of his rifle barrel stayed equal with his eyes. His muscles and nerves were drawn taut into his gnashing teeth and white-knuckled grip on his rifle. He bent over from the weight of his rucksack and hunched forward, panting for breath. He opened his mouth to suck in air, then ground his teeth when he let it out.

Paul had long ago given up any idea of moving silently. It took too much time. If you wanted to move with stealth in the jungle, you'd only cover about twenty feet an hour. They needed to travel a thousand meters in two hours. Paul assumed his "fuck-it" attitude, then moved out in his "ditty-bop." It meant loose walking, unrestrained. Walking without any military bearing or presence. Paul "ditty-bopped" to remove some of the strain, and relied entirely on the disciplined, acute awareness of his fear.

He knew every repeated sound around himself. The scraping of his jungle utilities against underbrush, the taut voice of his rigging, the straining of his suspender straps hooked to his web belt, the slapping of the canteens up and down on his back, and the sighing of his rucksack clamped against him like a sail. He felt the shoulder straps tight and cutting down from the mast of his shoulders as he churned forward leaving a small section of trampled earth in his wake.

He let the sounds pass his concentration, which pierced the middle of his brain in a fist of fear that clenched all of him, his flesh and bone. All he could know or feel stayed focused into every other sound that now decided his fate.

The fist of fear that was the struggle within him was unbearable in its tension and pain. Every tree concealed a sniper. Every foot of ground had a thin trip-wire strung across. Every corner turned was an ambush. In the center of this fist of fear and struggle was the concentration of all of him, now committed to the task of creating or becoming death. It played over and over again the consequences of his every move.

Paul took a step. A snap, like a fist striking, slammed through his neck. He fell to the ground choking on his blood, the echo of a sniper's rifle in his ears. Paul took another step. The ground erupted underneath him, tearing him through the air. Paul took another step. A dozen enemy rifles went off, the heat of the bullets searing his back, burning through his shoulders. As he fell he saw the rest of the team going down. Paul took another step.

He led the team to higher ground, staying just below the top to minimize their outlines. At the other end, he eased himself down again into the darker, thicker undergrowth. He pushed himself through the sharp branches cutting his face, slicing his hands. He cursed each time he fell or got stuck. The jungle fought him, pulled him back, tore at him, knocked him down.

Paul held his hand up and halted the team. The next man passed the signal back and they all squatted in place. Paul looked at the compass again. They'd been humping over an hour but were slowing down. Paul had not veered from his course. He waved his hand to the second man, motioning him to come up.

Jim Rich, corporal and the team leader, made his way up to Paul.

"What's up, pardner?"

"I gotta go at it with the machete. You'll have to tighten up to me, Jim." Paul took a drink from his canteen, chewed the water, swished it around, then swallowed it with pleasure. "Ahh," he said.

"We'll take turns, Paul."

"No. You be team leader, but stay close to me, Jim."

Jim nodded. Paul slung his rifle across his back and pulled the machete from its sheath. He held the machete's handle with both hands, tapping the point against the ground.

"Okay, Paul?" Jim asked, looking at him closely.

"There better not be any of the fuckers between here and the hill. I can't throw this very far."

"I'll be right behind you, bro." Jim squeezed Paul's shoulder and turned to go back.

"Here we go. There it is," Paul said, standing up.

"Here we go. There it is." Jim agreed, then made his way back to the other men. The rest of the team stood up. Paul watched Jim turn around and look back, then turn and wave Paul forward.

Paul began to swing the machete in swishing arcs, grunting each time it struck. He went at it in a fury. He slapped the vines aside and hacked at the thick, dark undergrowth. When one arm got tired, he switched the machete to his other hand and kept moving forward.

The exhausting effort of his work dulled his mind. His fear and struggle burst along the keen edge of the swinging machete. Through everything that grabbed at him, tore at him or tried to knock him down, he cut a path with an even greater urgency.

After an hour he broke through to the bottom of a small, steep hill covered with dense elephant grass. He stuck the machete in the ground and sat down. Jim approached him.

"Good job, Paul. We'll wait here and then move up into a harbor site for the night. I'll go back and tell battalion and arty. You rest, bro."

Jim moved back to the other men and Paul watched him talk into the radio handset while staring at a map and looking around.

Paul wiped his face and took a swallow of water. He waited a moment, then treated himself to a couple more. A memory surfaced in Paul.

He was at Camp Pendleton, California, in final training before shipping out to 'Nam. He remembered how he tripped every booby-trap on the practice course. On every battle maneuver the "enemy" killed him. He would approach a hut, ease the door open with the muzzle of his rifle and step inside. POW! "You're dead, marine! Go sit down!" And Paul would go sit with other "dead" marines in a group.

He would walk the jungle trails and large rubber balls full of rubber punji stakes would swing out of trees and knock him down. "You're dead, marine! Go sit down!"

They had buildings, like a small mock-up of Hue City, to train for possible house-to-house fighting. Three times they approached the buildings on line. No sooner had Paul lifted his leg through the first window than he was shot. "You're dead, marine! Go sit down!" He'd turn down the first alley. BANG! "You're dead, marine. Go sit down!" He almost got in the first building on his third try. BANG! They made him sit down again.

On the flight to Vietnam Paul had lost all hope. He figured he'd last about a day. Maybe.

Now he sat on the ground by himself, alive. It was the end of May, 1969. He had survived nine months in the bush and twenty-eight long-range patrols. He had survived the snipers and the ambushes. He had spotted and averted areas he knew were booby-trapped. He trusted the chills that ran up his spine. The men trusted him.

Jim made his way back to Paul.

"Are you ready to climb the hill now, Paul?"

"Yeah, I walk through the deaths I am. I cover ground."

Jim looked at Paul but did not answer. Paul took a long swallow from his canteen.

"Sure, Jim, I'm ready to take every step." Paul stood up and placed the machete back in its sheath. He reached behind and unslung his rifle. It felt good in his hands. He swung the strap over his shoulder and braced into it, pulling it closer to his body.

"I don't like sittin' too long," Paul said. "Let's move!"

Paul swung the muzzle of his rifle toward the steep hill. He focused himself into his fear, took a deep breath and carefully stepped over a bush, planting his foot firmly on the other side. He looked back at Jim with intense eyes, let out his breath and gingerly stepped across. Jim watched him curiously. Paul nodded to Jim, then turned, his teeth clenched in an anguished grimace.

He began climbing the hill with long strides.

Nicky Martinez

Nicky Martinez was a born leader. His strength lay in the fact that he had an uncanny ability to listen, especially to the gripes and problems of the other men in his recon team, and he could sympathize and solve those problems. He was a small, gaunt, stooped-over young corporal from the South Bronx of New York City. He was a team leader and a fierce warrior in combat, having been decorated many times in the two years he had fought the war in Vietnam. He had sixty-seven patrols, the most in the entire battalion. And he had a problem. He was a heroin addict.

Nicky could never go home. His five-dollar-a-day habit in Vietnam, with smack almost one hundred percent pure, would be five hundred dollars a day back in the world of cut shit, twenty percent pure if that. After his first tour ended he volunteered to extend for six months, went home on leave for thirty days, came back with a bad case of the shakes, extended for another six months, repeated and now was getting ready to extend for the third time.

He had just finished chow and returned to his hootch. He sat down on his worn cot and looked at the short-timer's calendars he had hanging on the wall. The whole history of the Vietnam war was there. The first one was faded. It was the outline of a beautiful nude woman with lines scratched to define pieces, like in a made-up jigsaw puzzle. In each piece was a number carefully colored in, running from 1 to 395 days. The second calendar, also faded and curling on the top and bottom, was a picture of another woman. The dates on the first calendar began in April, 1967 and ended in May, 1968. The second started in June, 1968 and ended in November, 1968. The third, a peace symbol, started in January, 1969 and ended in June, 1969. All those patrols, all those months, Nicky thought. Over seven hundred days in Vietnam.

Nicky had lost many men and kept himself alone and aloof from the rest of his team as far as friendships went. But he had become best friends with the sergeant of the 3rd Platoon. Nicky was a team leader in the 2nd Platoon and this sergeant would walk point when Nicky's team drew sensor implant patrols. The younger sergeant had proven himself in combat and they worked well as a team. A month before they had been in a mid-air helicopter collision in which both choppers had gone down. The pointman/platoon sergeant had especially proven his worth then. The two of them would get high together, the sergeant only smoking grass while Nicky would shoot up. Now his friend walked into the otherwise empty hootch.

"Hey, Nicky, how ya doin', bro?"

"Paul Timons, what a horror," Nicky said in a deep Bronx accent. It was the greeting he always used on Paul.

"I want to do my thing. Watch the door, will ya, Paul?"

Nicky bent over where he was sitting and pulled his footlocker closer. He unlocked the footlocker, rummaged around and lifted a sock, dropping out its contents. Out fell a needle and syringe, some cotton and a sizable bag of whitish powder. There was also a small "cooking bowl" and a rubber tourniquet. Nicky worked quickly. He tied off his left arm, pulling the tourniquet tight with his teeth. He put some water in the small bowl and added a good amount of the powder, then placed a match underneath and cooked it a little. He picked up the syringe, dropped a small piece of cotton in the middle of the bowl and placed the needle of the instrument in the middle of the cotton, drawing the liquid into the tube. Quickly he looked for a good vein, all the time glancing nervously at Paul. He found one and shoved the needle in, pushed the plunger and felt the rush. It hit him good and he fell back on the cot. The smack made him feel numb and blameless. He fought his way to a sitting position, stuffed everything back in the sock, placed it back in his footlocker, then closed and locked the chest. He fell back on the cot and tried to imagine bliss. Yes...peace. From his supine position he reached for his red pencil, stretched to mark another day on the calendar, and scribbled the day in darkly. He lay back and stared at the ceiling, trying to focus his glazed eyes.

"Here comes your platoon sergeant," Paul said.

"Yeah, well the fucker don't bother me." Nicky closed his eyes.

Miller strode in, slamming the door behind him. He liked to act tough but rarely ran the bush. Miller nodded at Timons. Paul led the 3rd platoon and ran it loosely. He never hassled his men. They were on a first name basis and Paul was always on patrol and on point. Even in the rear, when work details were handed out for the day, Paul would assign his men then work himself on the shittiest detail they had. Miller thought Timons was too young to be a platoon sergeant.

Miller walked over and sat on Nicky's footlocker. A dim light from a kerosene lamp was all that shed a pale haze on the scene.

"Don't get up," Miller said.

"I wasn't going to," Nicky replied.

"Would you mind excusing us for a while, Sergeant Timons? I have to talk in private." Miller wanted professional courtesy because he couldn't order Paul.

"Yeah, okay, Miller. See ya soon, Nicky. Keep the faith." Paul started out the door.

"Paul Timons, what a horror!" He heard Nicky's voice and smiled.

"Listen, Martinez," Miller began, "the CO wants you to see a psychiatrist tomorrow."

"A psychiatrist!" Nicky's eyes widened.

Miller looked up above the faded calendars and saw, painted in red, the bush name Nicky was known by: "The Stoned Killer."

"Listen, Martinez, for Christ's sake, this will be your third extension. Are you nuts or something?"

"I like 'Nam, Sarge," Nicky replied.

"How much longer can you walk the line? How much longer before fate runs out on you? You think you're immortal?"

"No, I like pushing it. Testing them, ya know?" Nicky wanted to sleep.

"You *are* nuts." Then Miller noticed the sleeve rolled up on Nicky's left arm. There were tracks of needle scars running along his forearm.

"You're a junky. Why don't you admit it?"

"Yeah, Sarge, I'm a war junky. Love to do that battle. Wanna see my record, boot?"

Nicky had Miller stand up. He pulled the footlocker close to him once more and unlocked it. This time he took out the medals, the citations, the commendations.

"Here's my citation for the Silver Star Medal," Nicky began. "Here's a citation for the Navy Commendation Medal with combat V. Here's a couple of Purple Hearts. Some Presidential Unit Citations. And here's a Cross of Gallantry." Nicky looked closely at Miller, his glazed eyes fierce now. "When you get credentials like these, then you come talk to me about my problems. Okay?"

Miller looked away. Nicky continued.

"Listen, if I turn myself in, the Corps will lock me up and throw away the key. They don't understand. I will not cold turkey in a jail cell. I don't deserve that. I don't deserve a dishonorable discharge. My bush record is the best in the battalion. You guys ain't got shit to say to me. Go away and let me be." Nicky fell back on the cot and closed his eyes. He was thinking of bliss and peace.

The next morning Nicky and Miller jumped in a jeep and drove to the psychiatrist's office. Down the road they raced, not speaking, leaving a cloud of churning dust. Miller wanted to get this assignment over with quickly, while Martinez just stared ahead preparing to face it. Miller parked the jeep in some shade and Nicky walked into the shrink's office. In an hour Nicky returned and climbed in the jeep next to Miller.

"Well, what'd he say?" Miller asked.

"He told me he would approve the extension, but this was the last one."

"Your time's running out," Miller said.

"You run as many patrols as me. You keep your ass here and fight as long as I have. You'd never make it."

"Well, hero, whatdya tell him?"

"I told him I love my country and want to fight to win this war. I wasn't lying."

"If that wasn't the truth, I'd turn you in."

"Why don't you start bein' a brother instead of a lifer?" Nicky stared ahead at the road that lay in front of him. "Let's split."

Miller popped the clutch, the jeep lurched, the tires spun in the dust and they raced back to the company area.

In the hootch again, Nicky opened his footlocker, took out the sock, went outside and ducked down into a dark bunker. The smell of wet sandbags and dank earth filled his senses. Below ground, Nicky smiled as he popped a shot of smack in his arm. The smack was the only peace he could find, bliss, as he called it, and the only thing that could control his fierce anger. When he was done shooting up, and the first huge rush of the drug swept over him, he climbed out of the bunker and returned to the hootch to lie down. More and more he wanted to close his eyes and not have to open them. He wanted to drift on his cloud forever.

With his eyes closed, he seemed to see and feel everything he heard. The familiar sound of the door opening and closing repeatedly, and sometimes slamming shut, came to him with the brilliance of a rifle retort. Men came and went, he heard ghostly talking, and Nicky thought it to be all those he had known who were dead. The voices were distant, laughing, joking, bolts on rifles and machine guns oiled to precision, snapping on chambers. With the rattle of metal against metal, like too many memories, the faces in Nicky's mind became transparent then blending, as though at the bottom of the South China Sea and sinking deeper, he had lost all sense of life, death or time. All the while he slept his restless sleep and thought it a nightmare he would someday wake from. Then Platoon Sergeant Miller walked in.

"Corporal Martinez!" Miller shouted.

"Yo," Nicky said.

"I'd like to speak with you a few minutes. Outside."

Nicky walked outside with Miller. It was drizzling lightly and a loose cloud cover held high in the sky blocking out the blue and exposing just a speck of sun. Miller spoke right up.

"CO wants you to bird dog a new guy," he said casually.

Bird dogging was when an experienced team leader went in the bush with a new team leader and just observed his handling of the team in the various situations that arose in the course of a combat patrol. Nicky had done it before.

"I'll go if you go, Sarge. Time you went on a patrol, don't you think?" Nicky said.

"Okay, druggie, I'll go. I'll bird dog you," Miller snorted back.

"You're never gonna learn. Man, too late for you. You just

don't learn shit," Nicky quietly replied.

"Remember, you're talking to a sergeant, Corporal. Don't forget it," Miller ordered. "I can get rid of you anytime I want, Martinez. You're a drug addict. You got the Southern Pacific ridin' up your arm. Express tracks. Case closed. Couple of years in a red line brig. Dishonorable discharge. I don't care how many patrols you got, how many decorations. You're mine anytime I want." Miller's mouth threw spit when his venom erupted.

Nicky smiled. "You got me! Anytime you want, you say? See you on patrol, Ser-*geant*." Martinez drew out the word "Sergeant" so it sounded long and important. In a cold rage that had beads of sweat dripping from his brow, Miller turned abruptly on his heel and stomped all the way up the street. Nicky let out a laugh.

The patrol was high in the DMZ within two klicks of the Ben Hai River separating North and South Vietnam. The new team leader was nervous and, with the addition of Martinez and Miller, he was going out with ten men. Too many for a recon team. More like an infantry assault squad. The new team leader scurried about as Miller shouted instructions at him.

Martinez did not use drugs in the bush. He handled it. If combat erupted he was on the right edge. Heroin was his only mistress, his only love. He could come back to her. He never received mail. He didn't even know where his family was. People would ask him "Where you from?" Nicky would reply "South Bronx." But it was as foreign to him as Vietnam. Now he sat calmly leaning against his rucksack, getting ready for his sixty-eighth patrol. He carefully camouflaged his face using grease sticks of green and black. He taped the end of his M-16 rifle barrel to keep mud out.

Now that the bush was drawing close, Miller was nervous. He kept looking over at Nicky and Nicky would look back and smile. Nicky was perfectly alert and ready, his nerves wired into the fusebox of his angry emotions. The warrior who exploded in combat.

Recon teams sat in bunches around the small grassy airstrip waiting as the choppers came to get them. Nicky noticed Paul leading his team across the strip toward an idling helicopter.

"Paul Timons, what a horror!" he screamed and thrust his fist in the air.

Paul turned and stuck his M-14 rifle straight up in acknowledgment. Then he and his team disappeared inside the chopper and they took off. Nicky watched the aircraft become a speck on the horizon, then disappear.

A big CH-46 transport helicopter inserted Nicky and the team. Everything was defoliated and quiet. Only a shimmering heat radiated in waves down on them, then reflected off the ground and rose in waves upward. As they walked quickly they repeatedly saw a white powder clinging to the browned branches falling off trees and to browned elephant grass that was flattening.

Nicky felt he was in a dream. He had been in this desolate landscape before. He remembered bombing runs in the Ashau Valley near Laos, then patrols through the wasteland, all the vegetation growing into death as if everything living had stretched to live one last time, then succumbed. Nicky could never figure out why there weren't any bomb craters. He remembered how he had gotten sick after drinking water from a small stream. That was on the second day, the day they found the rock apes. Over a hundred of them lay stiff and dead on the valley floor. They didn't die too quickly because, Nicky remembered, their eyes were closed. They must have slept into it. Whatever was doing the killing carried death into everything. Slower than a bullet or a bomb, but such a killing! No one had the slightest idea what was going on.

After four hours of humping two men got sick and began vomiting. The corpsman believed it to be heat exhaustion and suggested the team take a break. The new team leader agreed. Martinez approached them.

"We gotta keep moving. Try to hump a klick more north. Toward the Ben Hai. I've been up here before. There's more brush cover growing near the river. Here we're in the open." Nicky waited for a reply.

"As highest ranking man here," Miller whispered, "I agree with the team leader. Let those poor men rest. A half hour."

"Where we gonna hide? We gonna dig in? Hide behind some dead elephant grass?" Nicky couldn't believe these idiots.

"Just half an hour, Martinez. Then we'll move out," Miller said.

Nicky turned and walked away.

The new team leader and Miller watched him. He taped two magazines of ammo, one above the other, so he could switch them rapidly. He bent the pins on three grenades in order to throw them with ease. He settled himself in the thickest grass he could find and placed the three grenades in front of him. Then he dropped his ruck, lay down and leaned into it, the barrel of his rifle pointing into the shimmering heat rising from the DMZ's barren plain. He waited. Miller and the team leader ate some C-rations, as did the others, seeking what little shade was available.

Only Nicky lay under the 104-degree heat of an open sun. Soaked in sweat, he waited. He was frozen like a statue. Twenty minutes went by.

"Man, is Martinez paranoid, or what?" Miller said.

The first rocket-propelled grenades flew over the team and missed them. They exploded with black roars thirty meters behind. Nicky was the only one reacting. He fired a magazine, then switched the taped clips, rose to his knees to aim in better, caught sight of maneuvering North Vietnamese soldiers and fired the second clip, full automatic.

"Put out some fire, goddamn yous!" Nicky screamed. He stood up and threw a grenade, bent down for another and threw that. The team was in shock and slow to react. The new team leader sat terrified. Miller hugged the ground.

Nicky watched the smoke trails of four rocket-propelled grenades that slammed in like hissing freight trains. They impacted in and around the team. Six men were hit, two killed instantly.

The explosions sucked the air from Nicky's lungs, deflating them like a huge bear-hug. He lost his wind, felt himself spun in the air and twisted apart. There was a loud "wah-wah-wah" throbbing in his head and he felt mangled.

The four men not wounded and two of the wounded men rattled out fire now, strong and steady. They discharged clip after clip and popped M-79 grenade rounds in a semicircle from where the rockets had come. But all was strangely quiet. The radioman was calling for a medevac as well as gunship support and an emergency extraction. The men kept firing though no return fire came.

Nicky looked for his left arm. It was severed at the shoulder. Ten feet from him it lay, the tracks of needle scars on it, the fingers still twitching. Nicky tried to roll over to see the rest of the team. He could feel blood leaking from him everywhere. "Corpsman!" he shouted.

The corpsman ran to Nicky, held him around the chest and dragged him from the grassy knoll down to where the rest of the team lay. Nicky looked at his shoulder. Only shreds of muscle and ligament hung with ugly finality, absorbing dirt in the wounds as he was dragged back. His whole body smelled like an explosion. His jungle utilities were torn and burned around the wounds. The corpsman applied a tourniquet on the small stump still extending from his shoulder. Miller was also hit. The new team leader was dead. Miller had taken a piece of shrapnel in his leg. He moaned and rolled back and forth. The corpsman placed Nicky next to Miller and worked hard on Nicky.

"Take care of the other men first," Nicky said calmly.

"My leg!" Miller moaned.

The corpsman handed a battle dressing to Miller and raced to the others.

Miller started taking care of himself while Nicky's blood poured out with each breath. He knew he was dying. He did not think of Miller's unconcern for him. He thought of bliss and peace while the eternity of it was squeezing shut his life. His heart fought but was losing. His body was quitting and the sensation of it grew closer and clamped tighter. The corpsman returned.

He had only one morphine syrette to kill pain. The corpsman bent over Nicky. As he prepared to inject the drug in Nicky's remaining arm, he heard "Give it to Miller."

The corpsman turned and injected Miller. The sergeant became instantly calm and quiet. The corpsman dipped his finger in Miller's blood and drew a big "M" on his forehead.

The corpsman turned back to Nicky Martinez. In death Nicky's face took on the features of eternal peace. He looked numb and blameless.

R&R

I went to Hong Kong on my R&R. "R&R" stands for rest and relaxation, and you're allowed five days during a thirteen-month tour of combat duty. I ran the bush in Vietnam for ten months before I took mine.

I caught a ride on a chopper from Quang-Tri to DaNang. Then I got a hop on a commercial jetliner from DaNang to Hong Kong.

The runway at DaNang sped below me like a dark whisper. We climbed straight up, then dove straight down. A twenty-minute flight and we were there. A planeload of GIs with the thousand-yard stare.

I was really scared at first. After orientation and transportation to the Hong Kong Hilton, I locked the door to my room and sat smoking a cigarette in the darkness. Three days earlier I was walking point in the jungles of the Ashau Valley, hacking my way slowly forward, swinging a machete in sweeping arcs. It was hot in the jungle. I call those patrols "fuck-it" patrols because on point you have to sling your rifle over your shoulder and go at it with the machete. You make a lot of noise with no weapon in your hands. You don't stand a chance if the enemy is near, so you curse to yourself over and over and say "fuck it" and swing the machete hour after hour until time decides or collides or you're lucky and make it to feel the cool rush of the inside of a helicopter that is pulling you out.

I sat in Hong Kong trying to count them. Twenty patrols? Thirty? Flashbulbs burst in my brain taking pictures. Pop! The Cua Viet River, ankle deep in white sand, breaking down dried dead elephant grass. Pop! The mud hole of Con Thien, rain pounding down, walking out through the wire at dusk, hearing the deep rush of incoming enemy rockets, bright flashes bursting behind. Pop! Face to face with an enemy soldier, a ten second firefight on the floor of the Khe Sanh Valley. Pop! High in the DMZ. Pop! A mid-air collision between two choppers, explosions, pieces of rotor blade ripping through. Pop! Overrun. The killing floor of a slaughterhouse. Pop! Carrying bodies, the feel of them over your shoulder, that certain grip on the corner of a poncho, dragging them, lifting them, hauling them. Pop! John falling, a bullet through his head.

Jesus, I was crying. I couldn't stop. Sat there in the darkness of a fancy hotel room, the neon and glitter of life flashing between the curtains, and I was shaking and moaning like a baby.

I took a long, hot shower, the one you dream about for ten months in the bush, cranking the heat up, letting the water pound against my back, neck and shoulders. My spirit had so dissolved within me that I felt I could never enjoy anything again. After all that waiting and dreaming and hoping, the shower meant nothing.

I dried myself off, dressed and lit another cigarette, trying to decide what to do with myself. I still hadn't turned on a light.

Finally I got up the courage to go out, but not far. I made it to the first bar where I sat at a small table and ordered a rum and coke. Then another. And another.

I realized that all this time I had dreamt of going to Hawaii or Australia. I wanted to see round-eyed women. I was sick of the slant eyes, they entered me all over. They were glaring or squinting. When they squint you can't see them.

I wanted to go on an old-fashioned date with a round-eyed woman. I wanted to talk to her and have an ice cream cone and hug her when I took her home.

Then the vision of the pointman tracered through my head. I saw a ruthless ferocity lunge through violences. I got drunker.

I watched the main mamasan in the bar, she controlled everything. She sent a couple of women over to me and they sat in my lap, giggled and had me buy them drinks. I was bored. I'd buy them a few drinks then send them back. The main mamasan was becoming very upset with me. Giving me stern looks.

I looked away from her and saw a tall oriental woman. She was taller than me, her features smooth and polished. Her waistlength black hair was tied back in a ponytail. She wasn't dressed in a miniskirt like the others. She had on a beautiful blue silk dress that swept to the floor. I was captivated by her. I stared. I could tell she was aware of me looking, but she seemed shy, leaning against a wall stirring her drink, not acting like she wanted to be picked up. I don't know how long I stared at her. I yearned to dream in her, swim in her, go under, drown in her gaze and climb the summit of her being.

I have felt my heart explode in combat or cave in on itself while enduring endless enemy fire. I have shaken with a clenching fright. But the quiver to the beat now was a different feeling. A pleasant pumping where I could exist forever. It was near closing time. I stood up and walked over to her. She sensed me coming and stood rigid.

"Hello, my name is Paul and I don't mean to bother you. I'm just here for a few days from Vietnam. Would you like to talk and spend some time with me?"

She turned and looked at me. For the first time our eyes met. Deep to the spirit her dark eyes sank. Deep I sank with them. She looked me over closely, as if she were doing the buying, eyeing me up and down, trying to figure out if I was worth it. Then she smiled.

"My name Carla Wong. You army, Paul?"

"No, marines."

"I don't usually go out with marines."

"Oh well, I'm sorry, it was nice talking to you." I turned away to get out of that bar, to go back to my room with the lights out, collapse on the bed and watch the flashbulbs going off. She stopped me.

"I go with you, Paul. You buy me from 'san. One night? Two?" Carla held up two fingers like a peace sign and smiled.

"I'll be here four nights." I raised four fingers on my right hand. "And four days." I held up my left hand and she laughed.

"You want to marry Carla, eh Paul?" She laughed, bringing both her hands to her face as if she needed to hide her beautiful smile.

"Yes, how much to marry Carla for four nights and days?" I took a huge wad of Hong Kong money I had exchanged my American cash for, and put it ceremoniously in her hand. I bowed. Carla's eyes narrowed and she tilted her head to one side. She knew I was plenty drunk.

"Okay, Paul, but you let me watch your money, okay?"

"Take it."

Carla walked over to the patronsan and gave her some money

while she talked Chinese to her. The patronsan nodded, looked at me and smiled, nodded at me and I nodded back. Damn formal.

"Let's get out, Paul," Carla said.

"I see I still have a lot of money left. I thought half of it would be gone."

"We get this straight first, marine," Carla said. "I no rip you off. Okay? I be honest. You be honest. We get along fine. Okay?"

It was three in the morning when we left and Carla hails a rickshaw. An old man who looked like Ho Chi Minh came trotting up holding out the two wood forks that pull the large wheeled carriage. He smiled and nodded, showing rotting teeth.

"You ever ride rickshaw, Paul?"

"No, Carla, back home we mostly use cars and horses."

"You hungry, Paul?"

"Yeah, starving. Hey, Carla, can we get another bottle for the ride?"

"We go to restaurant first. They have drink there. What you want to eat, Paul?"

"Well, Carla, I've been in the bush for ten months. Anyway, I used to dream of Italian food. Got any pizzas around here? Lasagna? Manicotti?" Carla smiled and lightly touched my face. She motioned me to climb in the rickshaw. Then she climbed in with me, spoke some Chinese to the puller, or driver, or whatever his title was, and away we raced. The old man was fast, a hell of a driver. I would have liked to see him behind the wheel of a GTO roaring through New York City. That's the taxi this guy would have used.

He swung deftly through the traffic, missing everything by inches, trotting steadily, the rickshaw rocking. Carla did not talk to me during the ride, she talked in Chinese to the driver. Old as he was, he could carry on a running conversation while pulling the rickshaw. I was beginning to feel a sensation that seemed like happiness. It was strange to me. I wasn't sure what I was supposed to do with it. Clicking down the streets of Hong Kong in the early morning, riding with a beautiful woman to a restaurant for some good food. Talk and drink. I was wanting to embrace it all.

The rickshaw driver stopped by a restaurant and turned and nodded politely to us. He pulled the rickshaw next to about ten others lined up outside the restaurant. We got out. The driver looked at me expectantly. Carla pulled all my money out of her pocket.

"I know cost of ride. Not much, Paul. You believe me?"

"Yes, Carla, I trust you."

"I'm beginning to trust you, too. Do you want me to tip him?"

"Yes, Carla, give him a tip that's at least three times the cost of the ride. Is that enough?"

"Yes, Paul, he be very happy."

"Also tell him to wait for us. Tell him to keep his meter running. Tell him I will pay him well. Can he take us back to the Hilton where my room is?"

Carla spoke Chinese to the little man with the long white beard and his grin about broke his face. He nodded again and again and I repeated his nods. Carla and I entered the restaurant.

I ordered lasagna, manicotti and four pizzas. We ordered drinks and sat quietly, getting used to each other's company. When the food arrived I dug in, but was able to eat only a few bites of each dish. My stomach, shrunk from ten months in the bush, and living on C-ration meals out of cans and rear-area slop, had a private revolution. I got a terrible stomach ache.

"I don't feel too good, Carla. Can we go? I feel sick."

"What about food? You leave?" Carla hadn't eaten anything.

"Tell them to box it to go. We'll take it with us."

They returned with four full pizzas and the other food in boxes. Carla paid the bill and looked at me again about the tip. I shrugged my shoulders and waved my hand to leave it up to her. She smiled, left some tip money, then grabbed my arm and pressed close to me as we walked out. She held my hand gently. My heart beat that peaceful music I felt when I first saw her. I wanted to dance. But once outside by the rickshaws, I fell to my knees and threw up in the gutter. My guts were on fire. Carla and the Chinese men standing around watched me intently. When I stood up my eyes were streaming tears from the assault. I saw the boxes of pizza and food on the pavement.

"Any of these old men eat Italian food?" I asked.

"They always very hungry. They eat." Carla was looking at me different this time. She had many different expressions. This one looked like a quiet sort of happiness. I picked up the pizzas and gave one to each of the rickshaw drivers near me and waved my hand for them to pass it out.

"Our honcho driver. What does he like?"

Carla spoke to him.

"He likes lasagna." I gave our driver the lasagna. He was bowing and smiling again. The other drivers were doing the same. I bowed to them all, then struggled into the rickshaw, pulling Carla after me. She held my hand tight.

"Home, James!" I shouted, pointing my finger toward the stars. The driver looked up in the air. Carla spoke to him. He smiled and nodded and we raced off.

At the hotel, Carla said to me "Same tip?"

"No, give him enough to feed him and his family for a month. Give him that." Carla gave me a warm hug for the first time. Then she gave him the money and he came over and hugged me. I was really feeling good, despite the pain in my stomach. We walked into the hotel lobby and sat down. The sun was just streaking the horizon. The desk clerk was looking sternly at Carla.

"What the hell is he staring at?" I asked.

"Prostitutes no allowed in rooms."

"Well, I paid for the place so I'll just go kick his ass and we'll go up."

"No, Paul. No trouble."

"Listen, you're not a prostitute. You're a woman. And, Carla, I've never had so much fun with anyone." She cupped my face in her hands.

"That's why I go with you, Paul. I see your eyes. You see mine. Okay?"

"What now?"

"I go home, Paul. I call you later after you rest. Afternoon. Then we tell each other about ourselves."

"Aw, why don't you come up? We'll sneak."

"I have a young son. I go home. Take care of son. I call you later."

"Okay, I understand. I want to hear all about your family."

"I tell you later." She stood up and walked toward the door. I stopped her.

"Carla, could you give me enough money to get some food later? I might get hungry. And cigarettes." She pulled out my money and gave me some. She stuck the rest in her pocket and walked out, waving over her shoulder.

I went up to my room. Though it was dawn, with the shades drawn and the door locked, alone again, I felt safe. In the pale dark, I lay on the bed fully dressed and passed out. I don't remember any dreams. I woke up at noon soaked in sweat.

I called room service and ordered breakfast. Just toast and coffee. I didn't want to push it. I opened the curtains and stared out over the bay.

A cup of coffee, the sunlight through the window, ships in the bay, the ferry sailing for Kowloon. What an incredible rush to be alive. To live in peace. Not be edging death all the time, no ambushes, your heart pinned to the ground, explosions and rifles cracking. Screams of the wounded. "The wound, where is the wound, brother?" The curses at almighty God.

I stopped myself from punching the walls. My right hand was swollen. Not a moment in ten months had my mind not been centered in this savagery.

Then I thought of gentle Carla, kind and honest Carla, who would soon call me and spend the day with me. I lit a cigarette, lay on my bed and thought, yes, even those ten months at least brought me here. I got this far.

I dozed off again and woke with the phone ringing at 2 p.m. I hauled it to my ear.

"Hello."

"Hello, marine. This Carla. Want to get together?"

"Sure. When and where?"

"I pick you up in taxi. Paul, you mind if I bring son? It hot day. Maybe we go to beach. Okay?"

"Ah, yeah, okay, Carla, how long?"

"Right away, Paul. Right away."

I grabbed my camera like a regular Joe Tourist and ran downstairs. I walked outside and there was the taxi with Carla's dark eyes dancing from the open back window.

"Come, Paul. Hurry, hurry."

I ran over and jumped in the back. Carla hugged me and kissed my cheek. Her son, about eight or nine years old and already tall like his mother, sat staring at me.

"Nice boy, Carla. What's his name?" The taxi was weaving through the traffic toward the bay. Carla shouted to the driver and he nodded. She turned to me and smiled.

"His name Slim. You call him Slim. Okay?"

"Slim is a Chinese name?"

"No, Slim like American Slim. You Slim, Paul."

"Hi, Slim." I looked at the boy and gave him my best clown face, all scrunched up and smiling. Same way I smiled at the kids back in the villes in 'Nam. Slim smiled back.

"He like you, Paul. He no smile at many people. He no speak English, only Chinese."

The taxi let us off at a public beach and we walked out on the sand and spread a blanket. I had swimming trunks on and tore my clothes off and jumped into the water. Carla stayed behind, taking Slim's clothes off and putting on his trunks. The water was great. I just lay with my face to the sun and let the sea's rise and fall sway me. I almost fell asleep. After a while I swam back and sat next to Carla. She had her street clothes on and was watching Slim out in a little paddle boat that resembled a tricycle, paddling with all his might.

"He strong like his father." She stared after him.

"Ah, who is his father, where is he?"

"Hong Kong very crowded, yes? Not many jobs. Men tailors, honorable profession. Whore, bad profession." She gripped my arm tight. "You do what you do to stay alive. I do same too." Carla shrugged her shoulders and looked away.

"I fall deeply in love with my husband, Paul. You know, right? He come from rich family of tailors, Paul. You know what they do? They banish him to shop in Saigon. He be in Saigon almost two year now." I reached out and hugged her. She didn't resist, she allowed herself to sink deep in my arms and sobbed against my shoulder.

"When will he be able to come home?"

"I no know, Paul. Maybe never."

"I'm very sorry for you, Carla."

"How else I support baby?" She wiped away her tears. I

grabbed her by her shoulders and drew her back with me on the blanket. Her head nestled on my shoulder. I inhaled her perfume. A small irretrievable moment that would never leave me.

"You have girl, wife back home, Paul?"

"No, Carla, nobody."

We rested a while, then Carla sat up quickly and looked for Slim. She could not spot him and became frantic, jumping up and running along the beach, looking. I joined her.

"There, Paul! See, Paul! He way out! Too far, too far! Save him, Paul, please!"

I ran and dove in the water and stroked with all my might. Slim was, indeed, far from shore. When I reached him he was sitting in the boat not even paddling and crying hysterically. He reached out his arms and pulled at my neck, hugging me tighter and tighter.

"Okay, Slim, I got ya. You stay in the boat and I'll pull ya back." I push Slim and settle him back in his seat. There's a small rope attached to the front and I put it around my shoulders under my armpits and swim him back. Once I turn back to him and say "You're riding in the first river rickshaw." I show him my best clown face. He smiles.

When I get him to shore, Carla runs past me, scoops up Slim and hugs him and talks to him in Chinese. She takes him back to the blanket and checks him over very carefully. Then she turns to me.

"Thank you, Paul. You very good man."

"You wanna head out, Carla? Check something else out. I don't have a lot of time."

"What you want to do, Paul?"

"I wanna go to a toy store with Slim. Then I wanna get me a suit. Then maybe go to a bookstore. Slim gonna be with us tonight?"

"You come to my house tonight, Paul, okay? You have dinner with me and Slim."

"Yeah, okay."

We climb back in a taxi and go to a toy store and buy Slim everything he smiles at. I'm having a great time. I buy him a train set and a bike. Then back in the taxi and off to the tailors. I buy me a natty suit. Corduroy. And a hat. Then off to the bookstore. I wander, waiting for something to catch my eye. I see a book standing on display on a shelf. The cover shows a young World War I lieutenant in his uniform. I look at the title: *Collected Poems of Wilfred Owen.* I thumb it open, read some lines.

"What passing-bells for these who die as cattle?
Only the monstrous anger of the guns."

I buy the book and, as we're riding back in the taxi, read some of it to Carla.

"This guy's a 'Nam vet. He's one of us, Carla."

"Why don't you write poems, Paul? I think you be good poet."

"I'm no poet. Never wrote anything except a few letters. Wouldn't know how to begin."

"Your heart," Carla says, poking my chest with her finger. "Your spirit, Paul." She waves her hand all over my body. Then she smiled. "You be poet, Paul." We both started laughing.

"Oh, yeah, Carla, the collected poems of a pointman. They'd have to hold them like they wouldn't know if they'd explode."

Carla looked at me and smiled.

The taxi let us off in a run-down section of Hong Kong packed with people, every window with a line stretched across, clothes hanging and flapping everywhere, all the little homes packed tight together. Carla took me to a small second-floor flat. The floors were bare and there was only one room. She had a small table, two chairs, her bed and Slim's, and a small radio. For a prostitute, she seemed to live in poverty.

"You no like my place, Paul? I save all my money for Slim's education." I was thinking that she lived in a bunker a lot of the time, just like me. I walked over and hugged her.

"Your place is very nice, Carla. Thanks for inviting me."

Again she let me hold her, her head buried in my shoulder, our bodies touching in the embrace. My knees shook. Carla broke away.

"We eat, then Slim sleep. Then we have time together."

She cooked a great meal, one my stomach could handle. Rice and chicken. Afterward I smoked a cigarette while Carla sang Slim a lullaby. Her voice hummed a soft song. I recognized the music. That distant beating of my heart when I first set eyes on her. As I sat watching her kneeling on the floor, stroking Slim's forehead, I again felt that elusive peace.

Afterward we lay on her bed with all our clothes on.

"You tell me, Paul, about Vietnam?"

"No, I don't want to talk about it, okay? Let's talk about your husband." His picture was on the table, nailed on the wall and taped by the bed.

"I love him and miss him very much, Paul."

"Why don't you write the embassy or something?"

"I no can write, Paul."

"Get me some paper and a pen, I'll write." Carla's face beamed. She gave me a quick kiss and went and got the paper and pen. I wrote the letter to the American embassy in Saigon, telling them I was a marine infantry platoon sergeant who met Carla Wong, and the family was suffering undue hardship with him away. I pleaded with them to send him back. Then I sealed it in an envelope and addressed it for her.

"Try this, Carla, maybe it'll work."

She hugged me tight and thanked me. Then she pulled me toward the door.

"You go now, Paul. I see you tomorrow."

"Come on, Carla, just one night."

"You make some woman very happy, Paul. You good man."

I hugged her close, the tightest embrace I could manage, and kissed her once on the lips. Then I caught a taxi back to the hotel.

The next morning I had breakfast and waited for her. She called at noon.

"Paul, Carla. I meet you downstairs, okay?"

I went down to the lobby and saw Carla. She looked up at me when I approached, but did not smile.

"Hi, Carla, you feel okay?"

"Paul, you very kind. Kind me. Kind my Slim. Kind for my husband. I must say goodbye now. Patronsan needs me." She handed me back the rest of my money.

"Why, Carla?"

"I must go, marine. You must go. That is enough."

I felt defeated. I thought of the two days I still had left. Like walking the jungles, one becomes resigned to fate.

"Can you do me one last favor before you go?"

"Yes, marine."

"I hear they got good hash, ya know, hashish, with opium in it. Could you get me some of it before you go, and a pipe?"

"Yes, marine. Wait outside." She took my money back, then said "Can Carla ask one last favor?"

"Yes."

"Can I have address of you in Vietnam?"

"Sure." I scribbled down the address, my name and outfit. I handed it to her. She smiled. I shrugged my shoulders and struggled to smile back.

Fifteen minutes later she brought back a huge chunk of opiumated hash the size of a softball, and a pipe, and handed me the rest of the money.

"I won't need much more, Carla. Here, take half. For Slim's education." She smiled again as she took it, then hugged me for the last time.

"Goodbye, marine."

I went back to my room, closed the curtains, locked the door and turned out the lights. I stayed there the next two days lost in opium dreams.

The last night I was there I opened the window at midnight, stripped off my suit and threw it down on the street. I paced around the room naked. The time, the real moment was coming. The flight back.

I tore the room apart, drunk and stoned. Soaked in sweat, I snatched a mattress off the bed and held it up against a wall and punched it and punched it and punched it, until I finally fell exhausted and passed out.

A month later I was coming off my second patrol since being back in 'Nam, the heavy rucksack cutting my shoulders, bandoliers of ammo dangling, equipment clanging. It was a bad patrol. We were linked with another recon team and we both got hit. We had a fierce firefight.

In the hootch I grabbed my lucky towel and tried to wipe the camouflage greasepaint off my face. I didn't think I could ever get clean again. I saw a letter on my cot. It was from Carla.

Dear Paul,

A friend of mine is writing this letter for me. They're sending my husband home! The American Embassy contacted his family and maybe with pressure got them to bring him home to me. I expect him home any day now. I'm so happy, Paul! You were so kind, I'll never forget you. My husband or Slim either. Slim says hello to his favorite marine. Good luck to you! You are a poet!

With love,
Carla Wong

I put the letter down and lifted my rifle off my rucksack and gently caressed it and laid it aside. I looked closely a moment and saw two small shrapnel holes in the wood stock. I opened the flap of my rucksack and pulled out Wilfred Owen's *Collected Poems*. I read some lines out loud.

"Not in the hands of boys, but in their eyes
Shall shine the holy glimmers of goodbyes.
The pallor of girls' brows shall be their pall;
Their flowers the tenderness of patient minds,
And each slow dusk a drawing-down of blinds."

I thought a moment. My life was measured only by steps, and each step was my death. How many deaths will I have to go through before I can live again?

I took a pencil and scribbled those lines on the inside flap of the book. I felt like I wanted to write many more.

A Letter Home

July 4, 1969
Quang-Tri, Vietnam

Hello Friend,

I haven't heard from you in a long time. Did you get my last letter? How about the wood chest of glasses I sent you from Hong Kong? I hope they shipped them okay.

I, ah, I'm sorry if I came off a bit strange in my last letter. I got back from R&R a month ago. I guess time's starting to fly. Two more months left, or whatever. Damn, I'm tired!

Look, if you have to go to those anti-war demonstrations, wear a helmet. For chrissakes get yourself a gas mask from an Army & Navy store. I'm beginning to worry about you BACK THERE!

We don't hear much. Guys who voluntarily extended for six months came back from their thirty-day furloughs with all kinds of horror stories. One guy got beat up in a bar because he had his *uniform* on! Another guy's girlfriend waited until he got there to drop him. A friend of mine, Ted Willows, said he was afraid to leave his house! I mean, Ted has thirty-two patrols, I mean, Ted's received the Bronze Star and a couple of Purple Hearts! Whoa...Are you still alive back there?

We're fighting and losing everywhere! A million false fronts, with stampeding killers! You're one! I'm one! Either of us ever gonna learn? Yeah, they're gonna have to shovel the earth over us before they're done...

I want you to know I think I'm okay. My head is doing some crazy things to itself, just that things blurr at times, like a film going too fast or a 45 rpm record jacked up to 78...the sights and sounds go through me like that. At times I think it's a damn sight better than, well, slow...whatever that is...

I think the best way I can explain it is I used to keep up. With everything. Run a patrol with all the coordination and concentration it takes. Walk point. But my speed of thought has slowed down...I get confused deciding where I want to walk in the bush...I can't decide anymore. I used to go on instinct that had, with it, well, something else. Both of them worked together, got me through patrols, and through the shit...Now they're vastly separated inside me...in fact, I feel like I'm coming apart! There, you have it, fuck it, it don't mean nothing, it don't mean jack-squaddly! Fuck their war, and fuck their policies, and fuck their whole, I mean, they own the whole fucking thing! They control the whole fucking ballgame! What's his name, Nixon? No, no, Johnson? No, no ahh...Kennedy! That's it! "Ask not what your country can do for you, ask what you can do for your country!"! We all swallowed the whole mess with that one line. Never have so many fallen, so many been killed, so many been hideously wounded, because of one sentence! One utterance! Beware the ides of oratory.

I'll shut my mouth. The only thing I seem capable of doing anymore is losing it! Well, one thing sure helps. Hang on to your chair, or whatever...I've begun writing poetry! Yeah, out of my fucking mind, I know. Got me a book in Hong Kong, I suggest it to you...*The Collected Poems of Wilfred Owen*...he was a poet in the first World War, you know, the one to end all others? I can hold myself together when I read his stuff. It touches something inside me that I can cling to.

I've written a bunch of lines, and four or five poems. I'm sending you one. Don't laugh. Poetry is my last sanity! I must try...try to stay alive, my friend!

Peace,
Paul

BATTLE SURVIVOR

My brother is by my side.
Dying, he became my shadow.
His darkness clings to me,
And stretches across this country.

Clothed in dusky blood,
His earthen memory holds on to me
And stumbles with me.

Through the hollows of blood,
Scooped in screams, and spreading
Across this land,
That all day long we war upon!

For Timothy Baer

Paul was going out on patrol the next day. He would be walking with his team only five hundred meters out from Quang-Tri to set up ambushes. He was thinking of Timothy Baer, voices accumulating in his head like wind whistling through a skull's eyeholes. Everything his hand pressed against was a hand torn and cold.

He sat on the ground outside his hootch, his back propped against a wall of sandbags, his head tilted to the night. Paul wanted to write Timothy Baer a last letter. Perhaps then he wouldn't see him or hear him anymore in his head.

Three marines were leaning against the sandbags further down from Paul. They were passing a bottle among them and casting glances in Paul's direction.

Paul took out a pen and paper. He used Wilfred Owen's book to write against. Paul began crying as he wrote, and the three marines looked at him strangely.

From the place of no address
to forward your life to

Dear Tim,

I am writing this letter to say goodbye. I am very sorry you were killed. I was pointman on a patrol only a klick away when the firing broke out. I halted the patrol. We could tell how intense it must have been. I listened to the radio transmissions, anxious and scared for your team's extraction. I was frozen in a shroud of fear, and the spell could be broken only by an "all clear!"

I watched gunships fly over and use machine guns and rockets to rake below the ridge you were on. Then two hueys descended, one behind the other, and my hopes grew that everyone would come out alright. When your team was airborne, battalion asked for a casualty report. Your radio operator said "One Kilo-India-Alpha." I held my breath. He said "Echo-2 Bravo." I knew it was you, Timmy. My heart ripped apart in rage and grief beyond any human feeling I have ever known.

I loved you and realize you were much too good and gentle for the marines or that ridge of hill.

Yeah, bro, you were overweight. They called you a "fat body." I constantly worried about you from day one. There was something in you that brought out the worst in everybody else. They jumped right on you, your slow speech, your confusion.

Remember the mandatory volleyball games every afternoon? Before your first patrol I watched you miss the ball completely and fall down. You missed the ball every damn time and fell down a lot. I remember the laughing.

I'm glad we got to be friends, even for such a short time and under these conditions. I have felt a horrible guilt ever since that day.

I was third platoon sergeant and you were in second platoon. I went to the captain to try to get you transferred. I wanted them to keep you in the rear. Well, I know how much you wanted to be a recon marine, but I knew it would happen. I wanted you assigned to supply or cooks. I even tried to get you assigned as a chaplain's assistant. Yeah, bro, I know you're pissed.

One thing I noticed about you right away was that you had more courage than any of us. Despite the harassing (everyone said you were the slowest, dumbest kid ever sent to the jungle), you took every torture they could dish out. You defied them by not giving up. You ascended to a higher place than what was inside you that wouldn't allow your body to grow lean and strong, wouldn't let your coordination work, kept your mind dulled so you couldn't think fast enough. You had an undeniable courage.

They ran you up and down in the trenchlines with all your gear on. Trying to sweat weight off you and toughen you up for the bush. You ran until you dropped and had to be dragged out. I remember Taylor pinning you to the floor, sitting on top of your chest, slapping your face again and again as he screamed "You're gonna come with me! You're gonna get a piece of ass!" And you screamed back "No, I won't do it!" And Taylor slapped you again and I ran in and dragged him off you and knocked him down. Remember how Taylor swore he'd waste me?

After he left, you hugged me and cried and told me you'd be okay, you were gonna make it. Then you walked outside to take up your perpetual guard.

On your first patrol, the team came across dead, blackened NVA bodies, a dozen of them caught in an air strike. John, your team leader, made you hack off a head with a machete and put it in a clear gas mask liner and carry it and sleep with it cradled in your arms. I could kill myself for not being there to stop it!

When you got back, John and the rest of the team came laughing down the street ahead of you, announcing your arrival. And you, Tim, thinking this was a ritual you had passed, and were finally accepted, walked down the street like Caesar returning from your greatest triumph, the enemy's severed head held high. It was the first time I saw you smile. It was the only time I ever saw you smile.

The word was passed down the company street and among the hootches with great fanfare, and everyone went outside to see the next act. I'd been there ten months, yet I couldn't warn you, didn't warn you. John said to me "Watch what I got the fat Teddy Bear doing!" And I watched you walk up to the door of the captain's hootch while the cry stuck in my throat. And I watched you knock on his door like a butler, a big grin on your face. And when the captain opened the door, you held up the severed head and proudly announced "Well, sir, I'm finally gettin' a head in the world!" And I didn't do anything to stop you! I watched the captain pat you on your head like you were a good little boy, watched him laugh and go back inside. The whole company was laughing. Then John snatched the head out of your hand and threw it on the ground and kicked it. A soccer game erupted among the men. They kicked the head around, using all kinds of moves, until one guy kicked it too hard and it collapsed like a rotten watermelon.

You seemed so happy while all I wanted to do was scream "Tim! Don't!"

I fought back tears when you came over and threw your arms around me like a marathon runner at the end of a long race. All of you smelled like death, old death, rotten death. I guess it was then I knew it was over, for you, for me.

Before your second patrol I came up to your hootch to check on you. I tried to help, I felt so close to you. You were the only person I hugged.

It was a hot day, over a hundred degrees. I walked in and saw you sitting on your cot in the corner, naked, your head hung in defeat. The rest of the team was laughing, smearing melting chocolate bars all over your body. Your face held a grimace like death.

You weren't fighting anymore. You sat there accepting their judgment. I picked up an M-16 and screamed for everyone to back away. John said "Look at the letter Teddy Bear got from his brother!"

I read the letter. I remember your brother denounced the war and our government. And you agreed with him, Tim! And you wanted to be a recon marine! You were the toughest man I'd ever met.

Before John let you go to the showers he said "You better watch over me, Teddy Bear, because if I get wasted I'm coming back for you!" John's eyes widened and I've never seen such fear as was in your face.

Your second patrol was a bad one. Waiting on a hill for extraction, you came under heavy enemy small arms fire. The primary radio was knocked out and you were carrying the secondary. You fumbled with it, confused as to what you were supposed to do. John got pissed and snatched the radio handset from you and stood up to shout at you and into the handset, and a rifle bullet slammed into his head. The round struck him behind his left ear, spun inside his skull and stuck out over his right eye. He fell on you and, once again, you had no idea what to do. Other men had to come aid John and man the radio.

I was at Bravo Med when the chopper came in with John. The top of his head had ballooned like an inner tube with a blister in it. His eyes were fixed and the corpsman was giving him mouth-to-mouth. They laid him on a stetcher and a doctor walked over. "What's his name?" the doctor asked. I said "John." The doctor bent over him, looked at his swollen head, at the tip of bullet sticking out over his right eye, and said "John! John! If you can hear me, make a fist." Slowly, painfully, John's right arm lifted from the stretcher and his fingers closed in a fist.

They rushed John off. I never saw him again. They flew him out to a hospital ship, the Repose. A wounded guy from 1st Platoon came back from the ship several days later and told us they had shaved and cut off the top of John's head and went in there, then attached his skull again. The guy said John was in a deep coma.

As soon as I returned to the company area I looked for you. I found you sitting alone in the corner of the hootch. No one looked at you, no one talked to you. I tried. I tried to hug you. I only wanted to hold you close. But you wouldn't talk to me anymore. And you didn't want to hug me. I should have tried harder to get you transferred, to keep you safe, and I failed. I failed because I lacked the courage of my senses, or the shame necessary to do it. I was becoming numb with reason. I felt a horrible strangeness.

You didn't have the smell of death on you anymore, you had the aura. It hung on you like a body bag and you bore the weight of it alone inside you.

After the choppers were out of sight and the transmission of "One Kilo-India-Alpha Echo-2 Bravo" had stopped ringing in my ears, my team moved out. I walked point and every step I took was an explosion of rage. That was your third patrol. This place has that kind of evil. Your first patrol brought death in while you stood grinning. They kicked it around at your feet. You learned to live with it and sleep with it. Your second patrol took death out, returned it to the jungle for the kills. For killing was all it was about, Tim. Your brother was absolutely right and so were you. It was all only an act of killing. Your third patrol took death home.

I walked with an even greater urgency. I kicked out on point growling. Coming out of high elephant grass I burst upon a bomb crater with two NVA soldiers scrambling down the other side. It was like a moment of orgasm! A moment of pure release when I was able to squeeze the trigger and watch the dirt kick up around the two NVA. I backed up as I fired and rejoined the team. We lobbed grenades and moved out. I was right back on the job. I cannot tell you how much I despise myself!

When I got off patrol I went straight to your hootch. John died the day before you on the hospital ship. Did he come back like he said he would? Such a dream should not exist living or dead, don't you think, bro?

Everyone in the hootch was solemn. They sat on their cots and footlockers, looking the way you did. Yes, Tim, I know. They left you out there.

Only Tom would talk to me. I asked him what happened and he said you took fire like on the patrol before, and you were frozen in your position. When they ran for the choppers they saw you trying to get up, but you kept falling down. They climbed on the choppers and left you behind while you cried out and tried to stand and run. And the NVA advanced up the hill. I want you to know that I realize what you must have gone through. I see it all the time in my head. It plays over and over like many choiring voices until my skull swells and I feel blackened bone against my blackened heart pressed against charred eyes. I want the whole thing to explode!

I went in with the grunts to get your body. It was a platoon from 3rd Marines. Several guys were wounded and one was killed by booby-traps set up around you. When we got to you, you were kneeling on the ground, your hands tied behind your back and again to a pole they rammed in the earth behind you. Another rope was strung across your mouth keeping your kneeling body upright, your head pulled back hard. There was dried blood around your nose and mouth. You had been severely beaten, welts all over you rising in ugly mounds from your camouflaged face.

There was one bullet hole right between your eyes. And an empty AK-47 magazine left behind as a reminder. Your face showed the tracks where tears ran down your face through the green and black greasepaint. And I am lost forever in your gaze!

It was about killing, nothing else, and the survival necessary to carry it out. I hate myself for not doing more to stop it. There is no pity in my guilt for what I took part in and let happen. After you died I didn't want to kill anything ever again. If there is any "killer" in me now it wants to tear into everything that controlled us and wasted you, but it is all out of reach. The nature of killing takes its course that way.

I want you to know how much I love you. I wish I could have

gotten to know you better. I'm sorry you had to die. I hope you know peace.

I'm carrying the skulls now.

Peace,
Paul

P.S. I know you'll never receive this. Here's a poem I wrote for you, Tim.

MOUTHS OF ASH

Mouths of ash
Choking on the fire
Speak with tongues
Of smoke.

I speak in the dust of language.
I chant for the lonely bodies
Marching
Into their names.

Paul wiped his face and carefully folded the letter and poem and put them in an envelope and sealed it. He looked at the three marines who continued to stare at him. He lit a match and held the envelope above the flame until it caught fire. Paul turned the envelope in his hand, watching the flames, his gaze submerged in it. When it burned his fingers he threw it on the ground and stood up and began walking up the street.

The three marines looked at Paul as he walked away. They saw a lonely figure slouching like a sheet of paper crumpling back in a fire, pulsing, bitten away at the edges, with a searing heat burning into the finality of the center.

The three marines turned away. He was gone.

The Rest

We were on a "backyard" patrol. After we'd run six or seven missions deep in the jungles and mountains, the higher-ups would assign us to patrol for four or five days just outside the wire surrounding the sprawling complex of the Quang-Tri Combat Base.

Usually nothing happened out there, we'd take our cameras, snap pictures of each other, write letters, try to catch up on sleep. At night we worked. We moved into ambush sites, to press into the darkness until it was light. Then we repeated the procedure, over and over, then walked back in. It's like coming off the chain gang to shovel a little shit back at camp. It was a "rest" patrol before going into the jungles again. That's why we called them "backyard" patrols.

When we walked by, the marines with rear-area jobs were standing bunker watch. They had real serious looks on their faces while we swaggered out, almost in a hurry. We all smiled at them.

"Go easy, bros," one or two of them would say solemnly, and give us a fist salute.

Behind my camouflaged face I grinned. I was on point and walked through the maze of concertina wire and past the trip flares and claymore mines. I flicked the safety off my rifle and checked the selector switch to be sure it was on full automatic.

I eased the muzzle forward and dipped into the dark elephant grass. I heard our tail-end charlie, a black bro named Jackson, call back to the rear-area men.

"Sleep well tonight! Recon's on the loose! Swift, Silent, Deadly! Oh, yeah!"

I moved over a small hill, down into a gully, and tripped over the thick undergrowth. I began making my way up the other side. I pushed the muzzle of my rifle forward, cautiously, parting the tall grass. I tensed my body and listened to the hideous pounding of the shadows in my heart. I slipped, a dense form, a rigid ghost, away. I slipped through deeper into the night.

I felt ridiculous. Looking for a place to rest? I suddenly stopped. What the fuck was I doing?

"Why am I doing this?" I said, "I haven't been able to find a place to rest for the past eleven months."

Jim Rich approached me.

"Whatcha doin', bro? Why'd you stop?"

"I found the spot."

"Here?" Jim said, looking concerned.

"This is enough." And I sat down.

I couldn't go any further.

Remains

I've been in 'Nam a year. I'm getting short. But I don't feel short. I feel long, maul roars, exploding shells, death's long barrel, caught in cross-hairs, dead in a sniper's scope. And a continual falling of men obliterated in my eyes, with their final knowledge, their final acts where they died, forever in my breath. My body is infected with maggots and leeches. Snakes slither inside my thighs. Fiery explosions in my chest! I am rotting flesh stuck on the inside of a flak-jacket.

I cry every night. I cry for peace. I cry at times during the day. Peace for a hundred years, a thousand years! No more rifles' sudden bursts, quick flashes of flame, detonating thousands of rounds, winging past like supersonic bees, zing! zing!

No more mortars or rockets bursting! No more artillery booming or shaking! The earth crashing, shuddering...

I know it is very long through life, and faster and much longer into death, contained in the slightest movement, a hesitation, a gasp of breath!

I cannot walk point anymore. I'm exhausted from the patrols, I'm sick of the death of my friends, sick of the death!

I have ceased to be a fighting machine, a warrior. I am no longer fit to run the bush. I want peace! People at peace! Silence peace, solitude peace! I want to sit alone for hours and not have to listen to anything, see anything, feel anything.

I can't fight anymore. It's alright to cry once in a while, but they notice you're crying every day and every night, they get suspicious because you don't fit their definition of a marine. And a marine is all they want you to be. No other identity. When you identify, you live. They don't want you clinging that tight to life! Because after a while killing is done only to defend the dead. Especially when the war is over and you know you've lost. There's no other reason or cause. I couldn't walk point anymore, not with these thoughts.

What happened was the trip-wire I had avoided on all those patrols. It stretched across my path, hidden, held taut, by men. And when it exploded we all went down. They'll never give Purple Hearts for the bleeding minds.

I'm being punished for having bad attitude problems. They've labeled me a "malcontent." I accept the heritage. I refused to take any more part, there are too many voices in my head now, a lot of the time they all speak at once. It's terrifying!

My mind is a twisted body, coiled into every corner, stacked in piles throughout my brain. They are always with me and at times I feel the immolation of them in the flames. Diesel fuel and burning flesh, the stench blowing through the corridors of my soul. There are so many faces with fixed eyes, and the flies, bloating in the sun.

I have become only remains that will be sent to my family to identify, the sum of their love, the total of their son.

O the truth of war! The truth invoked in terror and rage, screaming and crawling across the razors, pinned down, that constancy cutting through me with sharp detonations, stung by black smoke, covered in ash!

I have become defeat and, with it, a defeat inside myself that runs in continual retreat, twisting in its passing, until I hang helpless at my limits, pierced by my fate. It is over now, it is over.

Like I said, I'm being punished. I'm up on a radio relay, isolated at the top of a small, high hill that overlooks the abandoned Khe Sanh airstrip. Low floating clouds hang like veils across it. Everywhere around the base looks like the surface of the moon. Shell craters, all different sizes, where each side pummeled themselves. Crunching into the earth with their vast iron jaws open and famishing! Then exploding in bright flashes that scorched with their snap, death everywhere upon this land!

I stare down the hill at the abandoned airstrip that lies still as a body at a wake. Inside my spinning head the silence is broken by voices. The wounded and the dying are moaning again, misted in the jagged, torn metal. Screaming voices rise from the vacant, musty rot, eating away the discarded flak-jackets. Feet crunch in dust, crouching low, then running. Their sound lifts with the rats gnawing the hundreds of abandoned boots. Hushed voices ripple in the blood-stained helmets filled with rainwater.

I hear it and see it where I stare. I listen to the pain of ruin rise and the cries "Corpsman! Corpsman!" race up and down in echoes through the trenchlines of my mind.

I am the walking wounded. I bleed to death inside myself. There is no place to tie a tourniquet, I am only able to ease the wrenching pain the best I can, with drugs. Sometimes I get some Darvons from the doc, and squeeze out the little codeine pill, separate it from the powdered aspirin. We call them "pink ladies" and I swallow three or four at a time. It's all I can do. My wound is invisible to others. My guts, or my buddy's guts aren't strung across the ground, both of us gasping at each other. They understand that. In war it's the inevitable.

But both deaths were born in me and nurture themselves on me. It's a slow dying. My weeping of blood where I cry alone on the dark trails and streams that have eaten their way through my heart. I am also that dead.

I cry as other marines walk by. Some look, others don't. No one comforts me. I am their distress, I am their deepest fears. I'm smoking a cigarette. The silence is broken by voices.

"...Look!...Listen!..."

"Yes, goddammit, I know!"

"...Look!...Here!..."

I begin crying again, staring down where Khe Sanh is buried.

"I'm tired, so fucking tired."

(((I drop my gear in a damp pile and throw my rifle on top. I see a glint of sunlight, a swish of instant, a rotation, come and go through my life for many months. The round clock ticking like a fuse, intent on its course, running through me to the detonation of my mind and heart. I recede under my skull cover, like a clip of ammo hanging in a pouch, while my nerves and body stay in the rifle's chamber locked and loaded.)))

Where was I? Oh yeah, me and three other "malcontents" from 3rd Recon man the radio relay code-named "Papa." There are also radios set up for the grunts. The very top of our hill has so many antennas sticking up it looks like a small house with twenty TVs going at once. A platoon of marines from 2nd Battalion, 9th Marines fill the fighting holes that form a circle around the communications bunker. They do what grunts do when they're not fighting or dying or dead. They fill sandbags and strengthen their positions, they clean rifles and machine guns and mortar tubes. They line up bullets and accumulate grenades. They talk to each other in hushed whispers or hurried commands, their eyes always darting about like wings ready to take flight.

I slowly finish my cigarette, inhaling deeply, blow the smoke out and watch it rise. When I finish, I walk back to recon's comm bunker. Outside hangs a sign that reads "Supreme Honcho In Tactical, Home of a World of Shit!" I duck down into the dusky interior.

Stokes, a wild-eyed marine who always wets his pants, turns and cackles to me.

"You see my new sign?" His fingers move nervously, picking at his cheeks like birds' talons, trying to tear the flesh from the bone.

"I saw it. Why'd you hang it?" I say, reaching for a can of C-rations.

"I hung it for you! You are the sergeant! You are the boss!"

I stare at Stokes while I open the can with a P-38 can opener. Gripping the small edge, I hack around the rim of the can and continue staring at Stokes. Stokes gets nervous and wets his pants. I watch the stain spreading.

"Be cool, Stokes," I say. "How are the teams in the bush doing?" I lower my stare to the open can where a coagulated piece of meat floats in thick grease. I plunge a white plastic spoon in, knock off a chunk and raise it to my mouth. I chew slowly.

Blake, one of the two other corporals, suddenly rises from the shadows in the corner of the bunker. He looks like a body waiting to be buried and getting impatient.

In this vast cemetery, full of processions and dirged marches, and digging and burying and digging again, among the hushed whispers and the strange laughing, the dead speak among themselves.

"You know what Stokes told me last night?" Blake says. "He said he was up here before and a big bear came up the side of the hill to attack and eat everybody, so he began throwing mortar rounds down, and finally one of the rounds hits the bear and kills him. He said he was written up for a Silver Star. What da ya think, eh?" Blake tilts his head back and forth rapidly, like he's trying to unscrew it. He grins at me. I stare back.

"How're the teams doing, Stokes?" I repeat, and keep staring at Blake.

"All's well that ends well. We only got two on our net. Desert Sands and Mongoose. The other three were hauled out. Slick time for them, slack time for us."

"You're a big bullshitter, Stokes, you know that?" I stare at Stokes and squint, pinning him to his seat. Stokes nervously turns away his face, picks up a pencil and begins tapping it on the desk.

"It's true," he says, "I wouldn't expect you to know or understand. I know it happened. I saw it!"

"You ain't seen shit, Stokes," Blake says, rolling his head around his shoulders.

I chew the last piece of meat, swallow, then throw the empty can aside.

"You're number ten thou," I say to Stokes.

"Dou mow wee," Stokes replies.

The last member of our four-man group, Corporal Schwartz, ducks inside and sits down on a jerry can. He keeps his eyes down and picks at his fingers. He glances up, looks at each face quickly, then drops his eyes again. When he looks at me, we stare a moment at each other. Schwartz has run as many patrols as me, and we both know it. I'm not sure about Blake or Stokes. Neither is Schwartz.

"What's new in here, Paul?" Schwartz asks, flexing his hands and fingers like he's curious why they're still there.

"Nothing, man, same old shit."

"Yeah, I know, I read the sign."

"Stokes here is gettin' the Silver Star for killin' a bear," Blake says. "He killed it by hitting it over the head with mortar rounds."

Stokes begins cackling with laughter. I walk outside and smoke a last cigarette before trying to sleep. The silence speaks to me again, its sound trapped somewhere inside me.

"...Remember...Listen...See it?..."

"Yes, goddammit, I know, I know!" I hiss through clenched teeth.

"...Look here...Feel it?..."

I begin crying, staring off toward the depths of Khe Sanh.

"I'm so fucking tired and sick."

I lift my head to the sky, tears flood my eyes and I can't see through the stinging.

(((I'm sitting in my hootch back at Quang-Tri, there's a .45 caliber automatic pistol next to me. I pick it up and eject the clip. I take one round and look at it closely. It looks like a tiny atomic bomb, like the one they dropped on Hiroshima. I hold it above my cot and drop it. I go "Weeeeee," as it falls. I pick it up again, pull the slide back on the .45 and insert the round in the chamber. I let go of the slide and it snaps forward, the hammer cocked.

I raise the pistol and place the barrel in my mouth. I take up the slack on the trigger. I hold it, looking at my watch. Fifteen seconds, thirty seconds. I hear the door to the hootch opening, and lower the pistol. Jim Rich walks in.

"Oh shit, Paul! There better not be a clip in that thing!"

I raise the .45 and show Rich there's no clip in it. He lets out his breath and sits down across from me.

"Listen, Paul, Captain Waggens asked me to talk to you. What's happened to you, bro?"

"I'm a war resister now, Rich. I burned my draft card!"

"I hear ya," Jim says.

"I've been confined to the hootch, Jim. I think the captain is going to shitcan me."

"Yeah, maybe. I guess you broke some rule."

"You gotta know the rules to break 'em. And we don't even know 'em. So what are we supposed to do? Call *that* a cause, a reason to fight and die for?"

"Whoa there, you're losing me," Jim says.

"They're all dying without me being there! Just like my best friend, Michael Bowle, killed in Hue! They're all dying! Goddamn!" I begin to lift the .45, then lower it again. Jim's eyes watch the .45 as it moves. He looks back at me after I put it down.

"Shit, Paul, you were the best damn pointman I ever worked

with. What happened? You lost it. You lose it?"

"Too many fuckups, Rich. The war is lost. The war must end. The war must be stopped. Now!"

"Well, I'm not going to argue with you. Whatdya mean, fuckups?" Jim watches me and listens intently.

"What, Jim, you want me to just rattle 'em off to you? You've been here the whole time with me. Didn't ya see 'em happen? Didn't ya notice, bro?"

"Tell me, Paul."

"Okay, dig, I'll just grab 'em as they come. Remember two months ago, when all the recon teams that were hitting the shit were coming back torn apart? Three or four of 'em in a row? Them guys blown away. They came back with their faces blown off! Someone finally realized they had mixed up the lot numbers in the factories, on the hand grenades, you know, the number on the five-second delay type, and the booby-trap type that explodes as soon as the spoon flies!"

Jim buries his head in his hands.

"Oh Christ! I remember. Paul, remember when we were on sparrowhawk and had to fly on a moment's notice, and having to check the numbers on the grenades? And still afraid to throw 'em! I didn't throw one for a month. Damn!"

"And Cory and John gettin' wasted in the jeep? When they hit the mine? And fuckin' engineers sayin' they swept the road? And the bombing runs in the jungle? The silent ones? Ever been around those, Rich? Eerie, I'm tellin' ya! Walk in, no bomb craters! No bomb craters? Then a week, a month later, you walk back in and everything is dying or dead. I mean vegetation, trees, rats, monkeys, all of 'em, Jim, that *normally* in a jungle survive! Anytime we booted around in there someone got sick. Didn't matter if it was summer or monsoons, bro, I mean I seen guys pukin' their guts up in the middle of those wastelands. What are they up to now? Can't kill all the gooks so they're killin' the land? Are they killin' us too?"

"Yeah, Paul, I've been there."

"Damn right you have. We have got to stop this war! It must end. Too many bros are gettin' killed for nothing! And I mean nothing! Nothing at ALL!" I punch the wall.

"Easy, bro, take it easy," Jim says.

"I've had it, Jim. It's over. They can do with me what they please."

"I wanna talk to you some more about this. I gotta go now." Jim looks at me, then at the pistol, then at me again. "How are *you* gonna end the war, Paul?"

Jim gets up and walks over and squeezes my shoulder. I stand up, shake his hand and hug him. Then he turns and walks out. I sit back down and pick up the .45.)))

I hear soft, muffled crying. I wipe my eyes.

The wind has picked up. I flick the cigarette in the air and watch the glowing tip disappear into the wind, sighing through the wire.

A Letter Home

October 4, 1969
Quang-Tri, Vietnam

Hello Friend,

This should be my last letter from 'Nam. I've seen the end. Done, done, done...

I'm coming back on a boat. A shitload of us are coming back, on two boats. The gunny told me it would take about a month. I'm climbing on the boat with nothing but the jungle utilities I've worn for the last month. I was up on a radio relay by Khe Sanh and while I was up there someone, or several, stole all my stuff. They stole my footlocker and smashed it. I found it torn apart in a bunker. My scrapbook was ruined, slashed with a knife! All my pictures were torn up. Money gone, mementos, souvenirs, letters, diary, poems, even my dogtags. All of it! Well, that's war...

A friend of mine told me Nixon's pulling out the whole 3rd Marine Division, which will leave all of I Corps to the 101st Airborne and the 1st Air Cav. Goddamn, they're good men! If the NVA mount a massive offensive I don't know if they'll be able to hold!

Why doesn't he just end it? Call for a ceasefire or something. It's gonna get awful rough for the guys left behind. But I'm out of it...gone...

Like I said, I'm coming back with just the clothes on my back. I'm ready to end it and it's ready to end me. I don't feel the fight is over, but I know now I'm ready to die in the fight for peace!

I was proud to serve. Yes! I mean proud of my life and my beliefs, before the loss. Since they continue to kill us, for no reason, I am more sane than ever. The 'Nam makes me saner every day! But the ones I think are crazy are officially "sane." And me, well, I'm "crazy." So it goes...

And you gotta know some of us are the biggest freaks going! I mean there hasn't been any party going that equalled the minority of us, here in the storm, listening to Hendrix. Oh so damn tired and scared, and still a little psychedelic lighting in bunker watch darkness. Big fat reefers burning. Just laying back and smiling at each other for a while...

It's the only way I can look at it! A good friend of mine, one of the last of the originals I came in country with, got killed the other day. At first they said he was a hero, spotted a sniper, shouted a warning and took a hit for his men. He was written up for the Silver Star. Then the word came from Bravo Med that he was shot in the back at close range. Powder burns on his shirt. Small M-16 hole through his back. Big M-16 hole blown out his front. The citation was torn up, nobody said anything. These things are...hush-hush...

So much is burning! A fiery determination! Something has a hold of this place and won't let go. Like a tiger with a bird in its mouth shaking it violently back and forth and snarling. I feel like that. I've been waiting for Dylan to write a song...

One patrol I was on we heard about the big festival at Woodstock. All the music and love and partying. We were only two klicks north of Dong-Ha. We spent the whole five-day patrol talking about hijacking an airliner. Just, you know, booting into Dong-Ha, going to the strip and hijacking a C-130 Cargo plane to DaNang. Then taking an airliner from there to Kennedy. Then order them to take us up to Woodstock. The six of us were gonna swagger into the middle of the hippies with our camouflaged faces and rucksacks and rifles and bandoliers of ammo and grenades, and grab a seat and pass our canteens. One guy had a bag of herb stuffed in his rucksack. I mean Vietnamese herb woulda fucked them up! Starched the critters! Stuck their arms and legs straight up in the air!

Then, can you imagine! All the warriors in 'Nam saying "Fuck this war! We've lost! I'm not gonna die for nothing!" And all of 'em, man, hijacking airliners! Paratroopers floating down in their chutes! Delta Company, 1st Battalion, 9th Marines, the baddest point company combat unit, (the Hell's Angels adopted the whole company as their mascot! really, they got a letter from them, this is legend!) they're nicknamed "The Walking Dead," can you imagine them strolling through the crowds, passing joints, laughing again?

Laying down their rifles, taking off their bandoliers of ammo, dropping their rucksacks. Sitting next to their brothers and sisters, dancing, singing, loving, welcoming them back! Not only would the war be over, but our generation would be healed and we'd all settle down to a peaceful life together...or something like that...it sounds good, like, you know, it would WORK! But, like I said, we returned to the war, because, naturally, we figured the concert would've been over by the time we got there...

I was up on a different relay a long time. We were starving! (As usual, the weather was too foggy for helicopters to fly something as dangerous as a food re-supply drop.) All of a sudden a chopper comes up on our net and requests flares, and says he's got a drop. We ran out and fired them and guided him down. He hovers just high enough to drop a message tube with accuracy. You can't fit a dozen fucking hot dogs in a message tube! We got three-week-old beards and whiskers on our faces, wearing muddy, torn clothes, looking like concentration camp prisoners, we reached out our skinny arms for the tube. I uncapped it and pulled out the message. I looked at the other men. One guy, Jerry, says to me, "Is the war over?" I read the message out loud.

"Congratulations! Man has walked on the moon!"

Yeah, it didn't make any sense to us either...

I've been having a recurring dream about the battle of Hue City. I never took part in it, I was still in the States, but Michael Bowle was killed there.

I am standing in the middle of a road that leads into the city. I stand with my back to Hue, the glow of fiery explosions, distant. On either side of me are columns of marines. They look tired, worn, haggard. Aged beyond repair. The dead on their way into Hue. With their sunken eyes and ashen faces. I do not turn around as they file past me. Instead I reach out to them, left and right, and plead.

"What can I do?"

"Tell them," one says, his eyes closed.

"Tell them!" another agrees, his head gone.

Then I wake up, soaked in sweat.

I can't figure the dream out. Maybe something to do with my poems and going home and the anti-war movement. I feel *their* strength...and continue...

Searching outside myself, I cannot believe I exist in such grimness. A scream in the night's penetrating voice! When I open my mouth, nothing comes out...

I'm enclosing a poem I wrote while I was up on the Khe Sanh relay.

See you in a month...you know, nothing comes near me now and settles but dust...I gotta get outta this bar...outta dodge! I am drunk with dying!

Peace,
Paul

REMAINS

This is the road I chose
As the road, too, made its choices.
I walked down barren lonely trails, that ran
Like bullets burrowing through flesh
Trails of pain, trails of screaming.

Finding this life, I've known what I lost
And all the years of my undoing.
I vanish in thought and feeling, here
Among the dying.

And I was all of father mother son.
And I was all times remembered
Of the love of man and woman.

The bullet struck hard, but I do not bleed.
All the battle entered me then, all the war.
I am decomposing where I stare
Across no-man's-land.

Look in my eyes, do you see home?
Never again.
I'm the sentry here.
I keep watch.

Land of the Free, Home of the Brave

Paul Timons stood again on American soil. It had been almost fourteen months since he had gone away to Vietnam. He stood outside the cheap hotel in San Diego where he had stayed after the docking of the ship that had brought him and fifteen hundred other marines home.

He stood in the morning rush hour, people dodging around him. One glance at his new Marine Corps uniform, one glance at the three rows of ribbons, then a quick glance at his face. Seeing how aged and worn he looked, they averted their eyes without a word, like mourners viewing a casket at a wake.

Paul was thinking about the ship's docking. The first thing he noticed, which caught an image in and held it, were cars. Thousands of them swarming at great speed, bumper after bumper. Across the overpasses in a vast sweep, into bypasses, through intersections, up and down every street. The roads covered, immersed.

There was something about the precarious thrust. Something about the acceleration of it that frightened Paul. It looked like very dangerous territory to cross.

It had all gone around, then around again. Paul felt dizzy. He needed a drink.

He walked up the street, smelling steaming hot dogs and the crisp sizzle of hamburgers. He listened to the whistling the tires made on the highways. He looked at the vapor trails crisscrossing the sky high, the jets' arc disappearing into blue horizons.

A bar was open. Paul walked in. He saw only one other customer, a man sitting on a stool, his head cradled in his arms, sleeping.

Paul sat down and the bartender approached. He was about fifty years old with a big belly hanging over his belt and receding grey hair above a rotund red-cheeked face.

"Just back from 'Nam?"

"Yeah, got back yesterday."

"Feels good to be home, I'll bet."

"Yeah, I guess so."

"I served in World War II. Pretty impressive ribbons you're wearin', young man." The bartender smiled cordially. "Tell me what they are." The bartender leaned forward on the bar, his head cupped in his hands for a closer look. Paul squinted down and pointed.

"This is the Marine Corps Letter of Commendation, this is the Purple Heart, this is the Combat Action Ribbon. This is the Navy Unit Commendation, this is the Meritorious Unit Citation, this is the Vietnamese Cross of Gallantry, aw, fuck it, man, I need a drink!"

The bartender straightened up.

"What'll it be?"

"I've been dreaming of a sloe gin fizz, yeah, make it two of 'em. No, make it three." Paul smiled for the first time since he'd been back.

"How old are you, marine?"

"I'm old," Paul replied.

"How old?"

"I'm nineteen," Paul said.

"Sorry, son, I can't serve you. It's the law."

Paul heard a bolt snap home. Then he heard a voice say "Sniper!"

"Listen, motherfucker," Paul began, "you see this ribbon? The Purple Heart? I got that when we were overrun. We fought all night. I got hit with shrapnel, my buddies were hit and killed. We were killing gooks everywhere around us. I mean, fighting those slant-hard sons-of-bitches to a goddamn standstill! They didn't proof me when they sent me over *there*! What the fuck's going on?"

"It's the law," the bartender replied.

"You know something else? I can't even vote. Nope! Shit, man, I can do two more tours in 'Nam, then come home and be able to buy a drink and vote, eh? Fuck you! Fuck you! FUCK YOU!"

"You're gonna have to leave now, or I'll call the police." The bartender was shaken and nervous. He acted like a shop proprietor knowing the man who will pull the gun. Paul saw his fear and calmed down.

"Sorry, man," Paul said, "sorry." Paul stood up and backed toward the door like a gunfighter holding everybody at bay. Then he ran out.

He hailed a taxi. A yellow cab pulled over and he jumped in the back seat.

"San Diego Airport," Paul said.

"Yeah, sure thing. You just back from 'Nam?"

Paul was beginning to feel like an oddly broken record.

"Yeah, got back yesterday."

"Wanna tell me about it? I've heard my share of wild stories. There ain't nothin' you could say that could be any worse than I've heard already."

"No, nothing," Paul said.

The driver drove on in silence because he had also heard not to press any of these men coming back.

Paul looked out the window and saw the airport. Yes! Because he could see the Marine Corps Recruit Depot on the far side. He grew anxious and his hands sweated when he thought of flying home. They drove on.

In a few more minutes Paul looked once more at the airport, with the Recruit Depot poised behind. He saw a sniper aiming in on him.

"Takin' us a longer time to get to the fuckin' airport than it took me to fight the goddamn fuckin' war! What's the problem?"

"Only one entrance I can get into. We'll be there shortly. Be cool." The driver turned, entered a road and they arrived at the terminal building.

"How much?" Paul asked.

"Fifteen bucks."

Paul handed him the money without a tip and got out.

"Good luck, marine. Welcome home." The taxi driver drove off.

Paul walked into the crowded terminal and bought a ticket. He'd be riding home in a bright silver American Airlines jet. He phoned the taxi company and asked them what the standard fare was from his hotel to the airport. They told him it was six dollars.

"Not even in the States a day. Two snipers and I got hit twice!" Paul slammed down the phone.

He walked around the terminal looking for a magazine stand or bookstore. Six long-haired young men, the same age as Paul, tried to sell him incense and flowers. He politely refused.

"Baby killer!" A voice rammed into the back of his head. Paul spun around.

"Who said that!"

"We all said it!" one of them replied, spitting on the floor to emphasize his point.

"Fuck you assholes!" Paul turned and walked toward a magazine stand to shouts of "baby killer!"

He bought a pack of cigarettes and watched through the glass, using his peripheral vision like he did in the bush, until he saw them move on.

He left and walked straight to the boarding ramp and waited. He was nervous and tense, his emotions ready to explode. He felt as if he were sitting on the little grassy airstrip at Quang-Tri, waiting for a chopper to take him into the jungle. There it is.

On the flight home, Paul finally slept. The humming of the jet engines, the terrific feel of being high above it all, lulled him enough that when he woke up to the "ding" of the seat belt light coming on he felt he had gotten the first rest he'd had in fourteen months.

Only his mother came to greet him at the airport. She hugged him and cried, but seemed nervous or distant. She didn't know what to say and Paul didn't know how to try. They shared only a couple of conversations on the way back.

When Paul walked into the house, his father came over and hugged him. There were tears in his eyes but he, too, was extremely nervous. Paul felt awkward. He went into the living room and sat down. There was the nextdoor neighbor, Mr. Jason, peering at him from a chair on the opposite side of the room. Mr. Jason had always been a wiseguy.

"Well, Paul, now that you're back from Vietnam, are you going to grow your hair long and become a queer?"

"Snipers!" Paul's mind screamed.

He stood up, brushed past his mother, scooped the car keys off the table, ran out to the car and took off.

"It'll take him some time to settle down," his mother said.

Paul bought a fifth of Southern Comfort, then drove down by the river. He sat there drinking it all afternoon and into the evening. When it got late, he drove to the cemetery.

He parked the car by the veterans' plot. He got out and began to cry with deep gasps and pounded the hood of the car.

He walked slowly among the flat bronze plaques, engraved with names of fallen warriors, until he found the one he was looking for.

Paul got on his knees and struck a match. He held the flickering light over the plaque. The inscription read:

Michael C. Bowle
New York
PFC CO D 5 MAR 1 MAR DIV
Vietnam PH&GS
June 9 1949 Feb 24 1968

The match burned his fingers and he dropped it. He prayed where he knelt in the darkness. He grew heavier and heavier as if a great weight had spawned on his back, something growing, wiggling inside him. He lay down on his back by his friend's grave. He stretched his left arm until his hand rested on the ground where Michael Bowle's heart lay buried under.

The last thing Paul heard was the wind faintly rustling the trees like a whisper. The last thing he saw before he closed his eyes were leaves toothed in death's gliding, slanting down on him from the branches of trees.

Paul closed his eyes and listened to his heart. It held a distant rumbling. He sank in his longing, sank away from the madness and pain and loss of his searching.

Sank with his friend. Together, they were home.

O as I was young and easy in the mercy of his means
Time held me green and dying
Though I sang in my chains like the sea.

—Dylan Thomas

Wild Child

August, 1970. Camp Lejeune, North Carolina. Paul walked quickly from the offices of 2nd Marine Division Headquarters. He climbed into a jeep next to his best friend, Eddie Macon. They had become friends with that kind of nearly instant rapport and recognition that ties men together for a lifetime.

Eddie was a spit-and-polish marine. He had never been to 'Nam, he was one of those left behind to be brainwashed. Brainwashed he was. When they both reported to the Ground Surveillance Unit, based at Montford Point, an area some miles from the main base, they first looked at each other strangely. But only a moment. Eddie had stood there in carefully starched and pressed utilities, spit-shined boots, a stiff utility cover on his shaved-to-the-skull head, while Paul kicked the ground with dirty boots. He wore washed but faded and wrinkled utilities looking like they had never seen starch. His creased utility cover was thrown back on his head like the cap of a ballplayer relaxing on the bench. On the point of their being completely different, they noticed at once. What lingered was when they looked into each other's eyes. It was a look that said "Yes, we've been friends all our lives, but are just now meeting for the first time."

A radio was sitting in the field in front of them. Captain Pelham, the CO, asked Eddie to get it. Paul watched, fascinated. A small, foot-deep puddle lay between them and the radio. It wouldn't have taken anything to run around it. Eddie went at a dead run, straight for the radio. Captain Pelham screamed to him "Look out for the mud, Macon!" Eddie replied "What mud, sir?" and ran through the middle of the puddle, splashing himself and soaking his feet. He ran through the puddle again when he returned with the radio. Paul winced.

Back at the barracks, Paul pulled Eddie aside. He looked at the shiny gold jump wings pinned over Eddie's left breast pocket.

"Hey, bro, my name's Paul Timons."

"Eddie Macon. Glad to meet ya."

They shook hands for the first time and smoothly executed the three-way handshake of the brotherhood.

"You Force Recon, Eddie?"

"Yeah, the badass and the best."

"How many jumps you make?"

"Eleven."

"Why do you jump out of perfectly good airplanes?"

Eddie squinted and looked at Paul oddly. Eddie was five foot seven, stocky and bow-legged. He had a handsome face, blond hair and blue eyes. Paul was five foot nine, skinny but very strong. He had dark hair and his eyes stared somewhere beyond.

"Recon's the best. Best training. Best esprit de corps. Now I just gotta get to Vietnam."

"Now, my friend, why do you gotta get to Vietnam?"

"What the fuck are you doing, Paul?"

"I'm teaching you what they didn't."

"You were in 'Nam. Who'd you serve with?"

"3rd Recon."

"Holy shit!"

"Yeah, holy shit."

"Well, okay, teach me, bro." Eddie had met not only an instant friend and brother, but a man who had actually been in the bush with recon. He was ready to learn.

"What'd you do with recon?" Eddie asked.

"I was a pointman and platoon sergeant and sensor implant team leader and malcontent. In that order."

"Damn, a pointman? Platoon sergeant? What the fuck's a malcontent?"

"A warrior who burns his draft card."

"You're a strange dude, Paul."

"Ya wanna get stranger, before I teach and you learn?"

"Let's go!"

Paul reached in his pocket and pulled out a bag. It was empty. "Goddamn," Paul said. Then he reached deep in his pocket and pulled out pieces of a bud of marijuana along with stray tufts of dust.

"This'll do it. First, my friend, we're gonna roll this up into what's called a 'bone.' Then we're gonna smoke it. I'll show you how. Okay?"

"Let's do it."

They did it and Paul drove them off the base in his car and straight to a Hardie's Huskies. Eddie had the munchies, it being his first time stoned. The hamburgers looked to him like T-bone steaks. Eddie consumed eight of them.

"Man, this is great. Wow, food's great. Turn up the sounds! You got any Hendrix tapes? Or Dylan?" Eddie was grinning and bouncing up and down in the front seat in time with the music.

"Have I got Hendrix! Ever hear a song called 'Machine Gun?' Off the 'Band of Gypsies' album they recorded at the Fillmore New Year's eve, 1968?"

"You know a lot about this guy," Eddie said, finishing his third milkshake.

"Hendrix is the *main* man. This is lesson number one." Paul put the tape in the stereo and cranked up the volume. "Let's ride!"

They pulled out of the Hardie's Huskies parking lot and screamed up the highway until the car was cruising at seventy. Hendrix's voice pleaded as he sang in anguish. "Ma-chine GUN, shoot my brother down! Down, down, into the ground." The sounds of a machine gun flew out of his guitar as he played up and down the strings. When the song was over Hendrix could be heard saying softly in the mike "Yeah, well, that's what we don't want to hear anymore."

Paul turned the car around and drove slowly back to Montford Point.

"Wow, man, *that* was the first lesson!" Eddie bent across the seat and squeezed Paul's shoulder.

"Yeah, that's the first lesson of many that you'll need to learn if you're to survive." Paul smiled at Eddie.

"I can't wait for the next one!"

"The next one I can tell you right now. Because it is all the other ones. Over and over again."

"What is it?"

"Don't go to Vietnam. The war must be stopped. Don't let them kill you for nothing!" Paul narrowed his eyes at Eddie, glancing as he drove.

"Whoa, bro, that one's heavy."

"They're all heavy, man..."

Paul sat in the jeep next to Eddie and lit a cigarette, staring at 2nd Marine Division headquarters.

"How'd it go, pardner?" Eddie asked.

"They're on to us," Paul said, reaching in his pocket for a joint.

"Lifers. They're just like flies. They eat shit and bother people!"

"No, the sergeant-major was a Medal of Honor winner. Iwo Jima."

"Holy shit, what'd he say?"

"He said if I was engaged in any anti-war activities against our government he'd pull my sergeant stripes off me. And if he could prove I was a subversive he'd see to it I got a dishonorable discharge." Paul shook his head. "Shouted at me. You know, the usual subversive communist shit. You know, Eddie, I had to kill communists for a living. Killed a shitload of them. And now I'm one."

"I think anyone who's fighting for peace nowadays, whether a combat marine or a college student, is considered a communist."

"Yeah, Eddie, everybody wants to end the war but nobody wants to fight to do it. A television poll can call someone up in their house and ask 'em, 'Are you for or against the war?' And they'll of course say, 'My God, of course I'm against that horrible mess.' But they're not communists, because they merely speak. They don't *act*!" Paul bit both ends off the joint and spit the paper out so it would draw more smoothly. "One can speak about anything. But if one speaks and *acts* on his belief he's a goner around here."

"That's lesson number 122." Eddie laughed.

"You got it, bro. Our manifesto!"

"One of us should be writing these down."

"I got all I can do to write the poems, to speak, to act. You write 'em down."

They drove off the base and halfway back were stoned. Eddie was hungry.

"Fuck Monsuck Point, man, let's get something to eat!"

"We gotta get back, Eddie, or else they'll shit on us. We've got the meeting tonight." Paul gave his deep stare several times at Eddie. They began howling with laughter and Eddie floored the jeep and they hit the half-mile approach road to the maingate at sixty.

The guard waved them through the gate and they drove down the street lined with parallel barracks, hastily built during World War II to speed the training of troops for the war in the Pacific. Montford Point now trained men for an assortment of duties, including boot cook, motor transport, supply and clerk, and housed the ground seismic intrusion detector team which they were part of.

They drove down the quarter-mile stretch of road and Paul imagined the thousands of ghosts that had peered from these windows, marched in these streets and had their guts blown right in the dirt in front of them. "The war must end." The voice would not stop throbbing its message in his head.

As they parked and got out of the jeep the deep smell of North Carolina pines filled their senses, and their being high accented the glorious fragrance of fresh-fallen needles. They looked at each other and smiled. They reported in.

"Sergeant Harris, we're back. Anything up?" Paul asked.

"No, you ain't missed anything." Staff Sergeant Harris was the team leader here. He had nine years in the Corps and went straight by the book. Always an order in his voice, always barking like a drill instructor. Paul and Eddie would laugh because when he shouted his huge belly shook. His eyes were always beet-red and it was known that he was a hard drinker. His wife and children cowered before him.

"What did the sergeant-major have to say?" Harris asked, more an order than a question. It was Harris who had seen a copy of a proposed newsletter Paul was working on. It was titled "COM," the initials of the "Concerned Officers' Movement." The movement stood for an end to the war, as well as eliminating the need to salute, and insisted that enlisted men had a right to fraternize with officers on their off-hours. This was not permitted in the Marine Corps, even though a sergeant and a captain might be friends. They could not get together in civilian clothes and have a barbecue or go out and shoot some pool. They had to stay completely segregated. Harris had turned Paul in to the sergeant-major.

"He told me he was proud of my combat record and of what I have done for my country. And he wished me luck in my last four months in the Corps."

"That all?" Harris's eyes squinted at Paul.

"I want to get over to the library and read his Medal of Honor citation," Paul replied.

"Well, it's late enough to go, but don't forget, 4:30 a.m. sharp we're outta here for a week of maneuvers. We'll be aboard the helicopter carrier Guam. That's it. Go." Harris watched with the slitted eyes of a mongoose as two of his prey slipped from his grip.

"Let's go back to the barracks so I can get out of this sweaty fucking uniform." Paul tugged at his tie, tore the knot loose and pulled it off as he walked along the street. He unbuttoned his shirt and tore it off. Several staff sergeants across the street stopped and looked sternly, but seeing the rows of ribbons and that the young marines were already disappearing into their barracks, they walked on. It was late in the day and they wouldn't bust any more chops. There was always tomorrow.

The barracks Paul and Eddie stayed in were single-story and more decrepit than the others. Cockroaches two inches long crawled and darted in dark corners. There were double bunks for up to forty men. Tall wall-lockers, bent, broken and dented, furnished the only privacy. At the end of the barracks was a little nine-by-fifteen room with three double cots and beat-up wall-lockers that housed the NCOs. Here Paul and Eddie, a corporal, shared the tight space with four other corporals. Two buildings were connected by a long hall containing the showers. This was all any of them had of home.

Paul opened his wall-locker and changed clothes rapidly. He pulled on a pair of jeans and a worn jean jacket with a small white peace symbol on a black background pinned over the left breast pocket. Eddie yanked a fifth of Jack Daniels out of his wall-locker and took a deep swallow. His face contorted and he passed it to Paul. Paul took a long, deep swallow, half choked and winced. They passed it back and forth. Paul offered the bottle to Corporal Dater, a quiet young man from Missouri with big ears standing out from his baby face. Dater smiled and waved his hand as if to push it away.

"Come on, Dater, get with the program," Paul said.

"No, I'll leave all tha' stuff to you."

"Okay, bro, just offering."

Paul and Eddie knew that Rich Dater was not squirmy or a ratter. He watched them with curiosity but never told anyone what he saw or heard. He was a true friend.

"What ya all up to tonight?" Rich asked.

"Got a secret meeting with COM," Eddie replied.

"You guys be careful. I wouldn't doubt the lifers are sneakin' round tonight, night before the big maneuvers."

"Ah, I'm not worried, ya know," Paul said. "We're both recon, commandos and all that shit. How these lifer assholes gonna catch us? Shit, man, most times we catch them." Paul gave Rich a wide grin.

"You ready, Eddie?"

"All set, Paul. I got the joints, the JD, extra cigarettes. That about covers my job, doesn't it?"

"Yeah, I got the papers, the documents, the stories." Paul checked inside the Marine gym bag he was carrying, then covered everything with a damp, smelly sweatsuit and zippered the bag shut.

"One other job you got, Ed. You forget?"

"Oh, shit, the tapes, the music. I almost forgot." Eddie reached in his bowed-over wall-locker and pulled out Jimi Hendrix and the Allman Brothers. He held them up for inspection. "These cover it?"

"Yeah, we're on the road. Let's go."

They walked into the night. Streetlights were on and there was no moon. Darkness comforted Paul but made Eddie nervous. After Vietnam, Paul could never be frightened of what the night could bring. Eddie was afraid of being jumped by the C.I.D., the Criminal Investigation Department, the C.I.A. and F.B.I. of the military, combined into one.

((The only thing that could scare Paul was a North Vietnamese soldier wearing a khaki uniform and pith helmet, stalking on sandals of silence, coming through the wire with bayonet folded out and extended on the end of his assault rifle, bursting out of the blackness with crisp flashing cracks from the muzzle, driving his bayonet straight for Paul. Paul lifted his M-14, his own ugly black bayonet extended, fired three shots into the onrushing NVA soldier and, as the soldier fell, thrust his bayonet deep through the chest bone with a sucking, crunching sound.))

"Paul?" Eddie's voice broke in.

"Yeah, buddy, what's up?"

"Sometimes you get spacy, man. Scares me a little, ya know?"

"Fuck it. Let's go, we're late."

As they drove off the base and turned on Route 285 headed toward Jacksonville, they fired up a joint and passed the bottle of Jack Daniels.

"Paul, I got to ask you something."

"What's that, pardner?"

"You gonna publish that poem you wrote?"

"I've been thinking about that, Eddie. If this gets off the ground, if this meeting is the real thing, not only will I print it, I won't use a fictitious name like the rest. I'll use Sergeant Paul Timons, USMC." Paul was smiling and wanted freedom. He was willing to fight for it and suffer the consequences. For all his brothers and his brothers to come.

"You got balls, Paul, I'll tell ya."

"Nothing they possess scares me anymore."

They turned off a side road and pulled up to a small house. They knocked on the door. Lieutenant Neil Jones greeted them and a rolling cloud of marijuana smoke drifted past their heads, caught in the breeze and quickly dissipated in the darkness.

"Welcome, brothers. Glad you could make it."

Paul and Eddie sat on a worn sofa. Paul's eyes hastily scanned the room. He saw a big stereo with monstrous speakers sitting silent in a corner. Six candles were burning, giving the only light, and the smell of jasmine incense filled his nose. There was an altar of some type on a dresser near the stereo. It appeared to be Buddhist, the Buddha in the cross-legged lotus position, hands upturned and gently resting on the knees. The serene face and slanted eyes seemed to be looking everywhere and peered into Paul's. Paul looked closely into them.

((Paul lay along a trail with thick, lush green fronds and bushes.

He was pointman and the rest of his six-man recon team, their faces camouflaged, hunkered down in silence, hidden on one side of the trail. The heavy monsoon rains were steadily pattering the leaves and the team waited soaked in sweat and water. They did not move for over three hours. Paul was cramped and slight quivers ran through his body as the water dripped down his neck and back.

Suddenly a movement on the trail was coming toward them. Paul took a deep breath and narrowed his eyes. Four North Vietnamese soldiers were moving cautiously up the trail, the lead man's eyes darting in every direction around him, his AK-47 leveled ahead of him, the barrel searching in every direction the eyes looked.

The four were now moving past the last man hidden in the recon team and, spaced about ten feet apart, they headed into the kill zone. Paul would initiate the ambush. His heart pounded. As the lead man approached his position, Paul looked closely at the slanted eyes that were alert yet serene. The lead man seemed to look right into the foliage concealing Paul. Paul stared into the eyes and squeezed the trigger, sending a fusillade of bullets punching with sickening thuds into the advancing figure. At the same time automatic bursts came from the other five men.

The pounding rain held the acrid smell of gunpowder like a pall over them. The four NVA soldiers dropped in twisted grotesque positions. The firing ceased as fast as it had started. Only silence except for the falling rain.

Paul jerked back as he saw the lead NVA soldier squirm, his legs contracting in spasms as he rolled over and looked at Paul. Now the eyes had a slanted dark serenity that held hatred. The enemy soldier rolled over on his stomach. His rifle had been blown from his hands. Paul watched with a strange curiosity.

The soldier began dragging himself on his elbows toward Paul. One hand was blown off and dark red blood oozed from underneath his body, running in deep rivulets with the rain, mixing with the mud. As he crawled closer he began making spitting motions at Paul. "Pe pe pe" the soldier's lips spat repeatedly in Paul's direction as he came closer.

Paul rolled sideways out of his hiding place so he lay on the trail, aimed at the spitting face and squeezed the trigger.

Paul waved the team out and they moved cautiously toward the bodies to search them.))

"You like my Buddha?" Neil was looking at Paul.

"Huh?"

"My Buddha. You can rub his belly for good luck."

"You're spacin' again, Paul," Eddie said.

Paul gave his head a quick jerk to the side as if he were a whoozy fighter picking himself up off the canvas after a flash knockdown. He shook it again.

"You into Buddhism?" Paul finally said.

"Yeah," said Neil, "Nishoyan-Shoshu Buddhism. Ya know? Nam-yo-o-ren-gaykeo."

"Yes. Whatever."

"Either of you good rollers? Roll some herb." Neil took what looked to be a pound bag of grass and threw it in front of them.

"Shit," said Eddie, "officers even have better grass than enlisted men."

All three of them laughed and they felt the deep trust of comradeship.

Neil Jones was a first lieutenant from Georgia who had been a chopper pilot in 'Nam. He had flown every mission possible. Resupply drops, medevacs, insertions and extractions. He had flown CH-46 transport helicopters. He sat on the sofa with his uniform on and unbuttoned. Over the left breast pocket were the Distinguished Flying Cross, the Silver Star Medal, the Air Medal with several clusters, and the Purple Heart. Neil had grounded himself ten months into his tour when, while flying as co-pilot in the heavy clouds and thick mist, he realized his pilot had lost his mind. This would sometimes happen to pilots in dark, stormy weather. They would no longer trust their instruments. The instruments would say the aircraft was losing altitude, was off course. The large black and white ball would be far off level. Rather than believe the instruments, the pilot would fly by the seat of his pants in fear.

Sometimes a pilot would crash into a mountain, the altimeter showing them at only 500 feet while the pilot thought they were at 2,000 feet.

Neil had to punch the pilot unconscious, then grab the stick and lift-control, and haul the chopper back to where the instruments indicated proper altitude, air speed and direction. At the moment he acted they were at 500 feet and descending rapidly out of control. Neil surged the engines, making them whine with absolute power, to gain air speed.

The helicopter just missed ramming into a mountain south of DaNang. Neil watched the dark mist blow away from the windshield while the bird just brushed the treetops on the mountain's summit. After landing, the much-decorated Neil Jones knew he could not go up anymore. He had not flown a chopper since, though he still wore his wings. Now he was the executive officer for a bunch of paper-pushing pogues. Neil had six months left to serve in the Marine Corps and, like Paul and Eddie, he wanted the war stopped.

"Now, let's get down to business," Neil said, drawing a deep inhale off a joint. "First of all we need to nail down our basic philosophy and goals. The Concerned Officers' Movement is first and foremost an anti-war movement. Our ability to exist and survive depends first upon our sworn secrecy. Second, we will publish a newsletter. I'm hoping about once a month to have two thousand copies distributed throughout Camp Lejeune. I know an officer who works in the copy section at main headquarters. He believes once we have the original material he can run off the two thousand copies. Now here's the rub. To really make this work we should use all Marine Corps facilities available to us. Hell, I'll even steal a god-damn chopper and fly at treetop level over the base while someone throws 'em out the back." They laughed.

"Like Chou-hoi leaflets. Ask them to surrender. Turn in their rifles and gear," Paul said. A huge grin covered his face.

"Yeah, like that," Neil said.

"What are you gonna put in the newsletter?" asked Eddie.

"I like to write political articles and satire," Neil began. "Paul has some stories and poems. Right, Paul?"

"Yeah," said Paul. He opened the gym bag and pulled out several newspaper articles from northern papers, a small short story by a three-time wounded veteran of Hotel Company, 2nd Battalion, 26th Marines, who had fought through the siege of Khe Sanh from January to March, 1968, and his own poem.

"Great!" Neil said. "You're on the ball, Paul."

"I'll write up casualty lists each month," Eddie said.

"Man, we're really flying now." Neil swooned.

"We gotta bury their principles before they bury all of us," Paul said, looking again at the Buddha. "This is the way I wanna fight their goddamn fuckin' war!"

"Okay, let's get the basics together," said Neil.

The three men sat around close together and talked in hushed whispers. Ideas were exchanged. Conversations about getting fucked, fucked, fucked by the Marine Corps and their country generated maddening talk and wild gestures. After two hours they were talked out for the evening. The three sat back smoking dope and drinking wine and bourbon in silence. An hour more and they were zonked to the gills.

"Woo-ee, what a fuckin' party," Paul said.

"It's near midnight now, we should break it up and split," Neil said, shaking his head up and down as if he were lazily agreeing with himself. "I know you guys got maneuvers off the coast starting tomorrow. Why don't you leave the articles and story with me. We're publishing this thing under assumed names. I'm gonna be Spider Man. Who you gonna be, Eddie?"

"General Smedley Butler."

"And you, Paul?"

"Well, I have a poem here that I wrote and I believe I want to test the Constitution as to my freedom of speech."

"What's that supposed to mean?" asked Neil.

"Well, publishing it and signing it Sergeant Paul Timons, USMC."

"You fuckin' nuts or something? Don't you know what they're gonna do with your ass when they read it and see your name?"

"Whatever they want to do is fine by me," Paul said.

"Jesus H. Christ, Paul, you're putting your neck in the noose for them. They're just gonna love the shit out of you."

"After voluntarily fighting for my country in 'Nam, being wounded, doing their killing for their reasons, I really want to take a look at this freedom I was defending and earned." Paul looked again at the Buddha. "Here's the poem. There's my name, rank and serial number. I figure I'm a prisoner of war and that's all the Geneva Convention says I gotta say to the enemy. They're supposed to treat me fair. It's their fuckin' Geneva Convention, it's their fuckin' Constitution, it's all fuckin' theirs and I'm sick of it!"

"Leave it with me, Paul, I'll have to decide. Using your name could blow the whole operation."

"Fuck 'em. They haven't invented a torture that could get any information out of me." Paul stood up, walked over to the Buddha and gently rubbed its belly. "Let's go, Eddie. Four-thirty is awful early in the morning." He grabbed his gym bag and walked toward the door. Eddie followed.

Neil gave them the brotherhood handshake at the door. "When you return," Neil said, "this thing should be ready to go to print. We'll make a final decision then. Okay?"

"Yeah, okay," Paul said. He disappeared in the darkness, his lean frame moving toward the car.

"Be cool, Neil." Eddie followed Paul to the car.

As they drove to Route 285 they could see Neil blowing out the candles behind drawn shades and the house enveloped by the night.

"There's a Dylan tape in the glove compartment. Play that, will ya please, Eddie?"

Dylan's nasal voice and tooting harmonica rang out. "It's alright, Ma, I'm only bleeding." They got back to the barracks at 1 a.m. and waited for the dawn.

Paul had just closed his eyes and started to doze when suddenly the lights in the NCOs' cubicle were thrown on by Staff Sergeant Harris.

"Four-thirty, you lazy shits, let's hit it." Then Harris kicked a large aluminum garbage can across the cubicle. The sound of its crashing jerked Paul right up and he dove out of his bottom bunk.

(("Incoming!" he thought. "Get your ass down. Listen to the guns. What kind are they?" He lay tight to the floor.

He could hear the recoil of large artillery pieces booming a distant echo. Soviet-made 152s. Their biggest guns. He listened to the retorts. "Boom, boom, boom, boom, boom." The deadly projectiles were flashing out the maw of the gun barrels and rushing on their way.

After the initial booms Paul knew that he had twenty-seven to thirty seconds as the rounds tore through space, hurtling in their dark arc. In the half-minute silence Paul was running through the night, trying desperately to get to a bunker. He dove into the first one which was packed with wide-eyed marines. The rounds were almost on them.

Suddenly the explosive noses caught the height of their arc and began to dive in their ugly descent. It was then you heard them.

"Sho-Sho-Shoosh, Sho-Sho-Shoosh, Sho-Sho-Shoosh!" They dove into the earth. Their impact was immediate and final.

A crack detonation, quick as an eyelid's flicker, crunched on them. The first ones hit over five hundred feet away. Still, Paul could hear the whistle of hot shrapnel whining and ripping the air, then a clunking sound as pieces fell out of the sky like rain and bounced on top of the bunker. The next three followed behind them. This time only two hundred feet away. Like sharp-edged, burning red knives, the shrapnel rammed the side of the bunker, making it shudder, and Paul and the other marines could hear the jagged metal trying to get them. The next three came in on top of them.

Like a large firecracker under a tin can, the bang was an instant eruption of earth, sod and flying shrapnel. Men screamed. The concussion blew through the bunker like a wave of heat from an atomic bomb. In that split-second, eternities took place.

Two marines near the opening were split by huge chunks of shrapnel ramming the bunker and racing inside. Hot blood burst from another marine in a surreal distortion as his chest split open. Then the terrible force shattered their hearing and the bunker collapsed on them. Paul and the other marines were buried alive.

Paul was pinned by layers of sandbags. He gasped for breath. He could not hear. His body was tingling as if the fingers of both hands had been thrust into an electric socket. "I'm dying," he thought. There were no moans, no cries, nothing but the smell of black powder and burned flesh.

Paul managed to free one of his hands and work it through the burst sandbags until he felt cool air on it. From the crushed and ruined bunker Paul's hand and arm stood up like a little flagpole covered with blood, the fingers twitching. Within five minutes it was over.

Marines who weren't hit raced from their bunkers with flashlights and entrenching tools trying desperately to get to the wounded. One marine raced by in the darkness and saw Paul's arm sticking up from the bunker. Other marines gathered around and began to dig. While one of them held Paul's exposed hand, the others dug rapidly. They freed Paul's face and he sucked hard at the fresh air.

"You're gonna be okay, marine." He heard a voice coming at him from a great distance. Then hands were under his armpits and he was dragged out of the dirt and rubble and laid out. He was forgotten as the marines dug frantically for their comrades. Paul's numb hands tugged at his ears. A sharp ringing had begun in his head. He was beaten and stunned. He passed out.))

"Look at jumpy Timons." Staff Sergeant Harris was laughing. "Get up off the floor, idiot."

Paul pushed himself to a sitting position, then got up. He charged Harris with a growl that came from deep in his throat, his face contorted like a snarling bear roaming the mountains. As his hands reached out to choke Harris's throat, Eddie caught him by the waist from behind and dragged him backward across the floor, holding tight. Dater and the others helped.

"You shouldn't have stopped him, Macon," Harris said with his mongoose smile. Paul was breathing heavily.

"I'll waste you, you worthless bastard." Paul peered into Harris with a warrior's eyes. Harris laughed again.

"Someday you'll make your mistake, Timons, then you're mine." Harris squinted at Paul. "Now the rest of you swingin' dicks get movin'. We're pushin' out in ten minutes. There'll be six-by trucks here anytime and you just grab your field gear and climb aboard. Now that's not so hard, is it kiddies?" Harris walked out of the NCO cubicle into the main barracks and repeated his procedure. Paul and the other NCOs could hear him raving as he moved through.

"Man, you were spacin' again, pardner. I was real scared," Eddie said gently.

"Someday I'm gonna kill that no good motherfucker." Paul's mouth threw spit and his eyes were wide and crazy. Eddie hugged him tight. "I love you, bro," Eddie said. Paul felt hot tears stinging his eyes. He bit them back.

"Let's get out on their fuckin' stupid play-war games. I got a few rounds of live ammo. I'm gonna waste that fucker." Paul broke away from Eddie and lifted his gear.

As they assembled in the street in front of the barracks it was still dark. The men were loaded down with full field packs, web belts with asspacks, and canteens. They climbed into the six-by trucks for the ride to Cherry Point where they would draw their weapons, climb on helicopters and fly out to the carrier Guam.

As they bounced up and down against each other on the rough boards of the truck, the sun was just beginning to break the horizon. It was coming up bright red and the sky blued before it, stretching back over their heads to where they could still see stars that were being extinguished.

When they reached Cherry Point, Harris peered into the truck carrying Paul and Eddie. The other marines became instantly rigid but Harris had eyes only for Paul.

"Feeling better, sweet pea?"

Paul pointed at the sun. "Red at night, sailor's delight. Red in morning, sailor's warning."

"What's that supposed to mean, Sergeant?"

"Think about it," Paul replied. Harris laughed and walked toward the other trucks.

Paul reached in his pocket and pulled out three rounds of live 5.56 mm rifle ammunition. He rolled the three rounds in his hand, caressing them. He smiled, opening his palm just enough to show Eddie.

"Holy shit, bro, you ain't kiddin'. You're spacin' real bad, Paul. I'm scared."

"Not to worry, pardner," Paul said. "I know how to use these things. The fuckin' Corps taught me real well. I know just where these things are to be delivered. This is my rifle. Together we are the defenders of our nation. I kill the enemy of my country, that's how they trained me. I see one, and the rotten bastard's a sniper. I know how to advance on a sniper. I know how to pop 'em. If that asshole gives me a chance I'm gonna waste his ass."

Eddie couldn't say a word. He felt empty and useless beside the eternal rage of Paul Timons. Sometimes, Eddie thought, Paul was like a wild beast, completely out of control.

By 7 a.m. they were climbing up the loading ramp of a big CH-53 transport helicopter, the biggest in the fleet and the fastest. They settled in silence because talk was impossible inside the roaring interior of the chopper. The engines began to whine and build power. The huge single-sweeping rotor blade began to turn slowly, then faster and faster, until it became a blur. Suddenly there was a lurch like an elevator going up, and out the window Paul watched the ground move farther and farther away as they rose up to one thousand feet and leveled off. The nose of the -53 dipped a little and he saw Cherry Point disappear behind them as they flew across the blue Atlantic toward the Guam.

Because helicopters need little room to land, the Guam was only about a quarter the size of a normal carrier. Covered by intense fighter-jet protection, the Guam could put thousands of troops ashore with a minimum of casualties.

When the CH-53 touched down on the deck everyone stood up at once and filed off the loading ramp in two columns to the whines and smells of engines, grease and diesel fumes.

The flight had calmed Paul down.

"This is just an airport," Paul shouted back at Eddie. "Let's go to the terminal bar and get us a JD." He grinned broadly.

"I wonder if any of these swabbies got herb," Eddie said.

"I think anchor-clankers are boozers, if I remember correctly."

"Whatdya mean 'if I remember correctly'?"

They were assembled by platoons now and stood off to the side near the bridge admiring the bright blue distance and depth of the Atlantic and relishing the strong sea breeze after all their marching and running through the boondocks surrounding Camp Lejeune. The swamps were the worst. Anything could happen. The marines hated them. These maneuvers were intended to train for a swamp style invasion. Paul and Eddie's team was to implant sensor devices capable of detecting the movement of enemy soldiers in a marshy environment.

"When I went to 'Nam, Eddie," Paul began, "they flew me over in a hurry. Coming home, they stuck me on one of these tubs for twenty-seven days before we saw the shoreline of California. Then we had to wait two days for our sister ship, all us short-timers crammed to one side of the deck all the time, just staring at the coast of California, watching in silence at night as the lights of the WORLD came on. Man, they wanted both our ships going in together. Just so Nixon would look good. Bringin' the boys home. Once again it was for them, not us. What a bunch of shit. Anyway, that ship was the Iwo Jima and she was a sister ship to this one."

"And the swabbies just got drunk?"

"I went on board the ship with two hundred joints stuffed in the bottom of a willy-peter bag. I had copped them from a mamasan in Quang-Tri City before leaving. By the time we hit California twenty-seven days later they were all gone. All of 'em, man. Every night gyrenes and swabbies gathered together because, ah, as you know, a ship is like a small town and good news travels fast. Anyway, we all got along just great. None of this horseshit they force-feed you in boot camp how marines and navy always fight. That's a big bunch of shit they stick on your boots. Truth is I felt a tight brotherhood with them. If the wind was blowing to the stern we met at the stern. If the wind was blowing to the bow we met up by the bow. Starboard wind, starboard stonies. Port wind, partyed pardners. We figured it out real quick and had some great belly-laughing times. But the goddamn swabbies only had the booze. Too scared of inspections, I guess. So I drained their bottles and they sucked my bones. Dig, man, we PARTYED!"

Staff Sergeant Harris stood in front of the assembled marines. "The chief here," pointing to a middle-aged sailor with the cracks of a windy sea already crevicing out from his eyes, "will take you all below and show you your quarters. I do not want any bitching. We're guests of the Navy on this ship and you will all conduct yourselves accordingly. Understand?" The marines remained silent. Harris turned and walked briskly away across the deck.

"My name's Chief Peters and I want to welcome you all aboard. I have always had the greatest admiration for you marines. I know how you guys get the dirty work. So I'll try to make your stay as comfortable as possible under the circumstances." He sucked in another lungful of air. "You're going to find the quarters cramped but there is nothing you or I can do about that. Once you're settled feel free to roam the ship except for the flight deck, the elevator lifts where the personnel are working and, most of all, and don't forget, stay clear of the bridge under any circumstances. We serve good hot chow here, which I believe you'll enjoy." He smiled with warmth. "I also know how you guys have to eat out of cans all the time. I've tasted that C-ration slop, made me throw up." He made a wretching motion grabbing at his throat. The men relaxed and laughed.

Someone in the third row shouted "Whatdya get, Chief, the ham and motherfuckers?" Everyone cracked up, including the chief.

"Let's not have a Laugh-In here," Peters said. "Follow me below in single file and I'll stow you sea-going bellhops away in your new home for the next seven days. Oh, yeah, every night there's a movie below decks starting at 1930 hours. And we got a PX and cafeteria, a snack bar and a library, but I don't think any of ya's will be there." Again, the broad grin.

Another voice rang out from within the columns of men. "Where's the babes? Where's the foxes?" Another shouted "Where's the bar? Fer Chrissakes, Chief, give us some important information."

The chief led them toward a hatch opening to a walkway with tight descending metal stairs. The marines grunted and cursed as they tried to make it through the narrow corridors and passageways with their bulky gear. They got settled in their tight space. They lay in their berths quietly for two hours lulled by the shifting sea that calmly held the ship in its aqueous grip and rocked it as it lay still in the water.

Below decks, where the marines were stowed away, the heat built rapidly. There were no portholes and ventilation was poor. They lay soaked in sweat. True to Harris's command, they did not bitch.

About mid-afternoon their CO, Captain Pelham, entered with Staff Sergeant Harris. Pelham was a mustanger, a career non-com who had risen to master sergeant and been given a temporary commission as second lieutenant during the Tet offensive of 1968. He was happy to be an officer, though he could not be promoted beyond captain. After twenty-one years in a supply battalion, he had finally been given a field command though he had no overseas duty. He tried to be a good leader.

Of the twenty-five men assigned to Pelham's command only Paul Timons had handled the sensor devices in combat. Pelham forgave Paul his being a poor garrison marine. He valued his field advice and expertise with a map, compass and radio.

"How are you men doing?" Pelham had a soft, fleshy face and a small beer gut. He spoke softly and there was gentleness in his eyes. He smiled and looked from one face to another.

"Fine, sir," several marines replied.

"Need women and a slop-chute, sir," Eddie said with a grin.

"You can get that back at Jacksonville, Corporal Macon. Right now we have an important job to do."

"What important job?" Paul lifted his head from the pillow it was resting on and stared at the captain. The captain never knew what kind of answer Timons was expecting.

"Sergeant, you handled the sensor devices in combat. Did you ever run an implant patrol under swampy conditions?"

"Hell no, Captain."

"Well, tomorrow you will." Captain Pelham was searching for a reason. His fingers rubbed hard on his chin and he could not understand why this buck sergeant made him feel so nervous.

Paul picked up his rifle, sat back and began working the bolt.

"You should be happy this is just practice," Harris interjected.

"You gonna lead us, Sergeant Harris?" Paul tilted his head to one side and intently watched Harris.

"Maybe that's none of your damn business, Sergeant. Maybe I'm starting to get tired of your shit, Sergeant. Who the fuck you think you are? How come you act so cocky out here and in the rear you're not worth a fiddler's fuck?" Harris was snarling out the words. He started screaming. "Sergeant, do you know how goddamn fucking mad you make me? Do you have any idea how you ruin every fucking one of my days? I'd give my left nut to see you shipped back to 'Nam. Your record don't mean jack-squaddly to me. Are you listening to me, Sergeant?"

Captain Pelham turned to Harris and gripped his forearm with his hand. "Let's keep cool heads here," he said.

Paul sat on the cot gripping his rifle. He lifted the barrel so it pointed at Harris's crotch. He pulled the trigger and heard the firing pin ram home on an empty chamber. Marines were trying to suppress laughs.

Harris began shaking his head up and down, faster and faster, as if he were in touch with something inside it. "You motherfucker" was all he said. Then he looked at Pelham.

"Begging the captain's permission, sir, I'm going to wait outside before I bash this fucking sorry example of civilian shit right in his cocksucking head." He turned and left.

"What is your problem, Sergeant?" Captain Pelham crossed his arms on his chest and looked at Paul. He couldn't figure out why he liked this brash young sergeant. Still, he had to handle this like a captain, and a buck sergeant had no rights with either a staff sergeant or a captain.

"You have four months left, Sergeant, and your ass is goin' to end up in the can. Why can't you square yourself away? What is your problem?"

"I don't have many problems, Captain," Paul began, the adrenalin pumping hard in his ears, the constant ringing getting louder. "But maybe I have a few."

"Well, we're a big, happy family. Share them with us."

"I'm sick of not being free. I can't stand not being able to feel freedom. We're going into swamps on some rinky-dink operation. I never saw swamps like these in 'Nam. Northern fucking I Corps. Triple canopy jungle and mountains. Long irregular valleys in between. Monsoons. Rain, fucking rain, day and night, day and night. Then heat that'll cook your ass in five minutes of humping, but you hump all day. I want to be free. I want this goddamn military machine ground to a halt. I want us all to be free. What the fuck did I fight for? I'll tell you. Nothing. We've been losing the war since we started. Which of these men goes over next and comes home in a glad bag? What the fuck are we practicing for? The sniper's bullet? The land mine? The 122 mm rockets? The ambushes? Which of these men are being trained properly for that?" Paul lowered his head and looked away. "You wanna practice war, Captain? Fly with us into a hot LZ. Have AK-47s and MGs cracking in an interlocking crossfire. Hit the deck, drag the wounded. There is only one rule. One thing and one thing only you can do in war. Fight your ass off. Period. You get through it no other way. So what's to practice for? Let's put our toys down and go home. I want the war ended. I want to be free."

"You'll be free in four months, Sergeant. Can't you make that after all you've been through?"

"For all I've been through and my brothers have been through and my brothers to come will be going through, I want us to be free now, I want to be free as a marine veteran, a sergeant, I want to feel free right now. Why should I have to wait? I put my life on the line again and again as a defender of freedom. Why do I feel like a prisoner?" Paul looked up. "Yeah, I know, I'm crazy."

"No, Sergeant," Captain Pelham said softly, "you're not crazy. Perhaps you make too much sense. I'm ordered to do it. I order you men to do it. Shit flows downhill. I could use your help on this one, Sergeant Timons. I would really appreciate it if you would come to the officers' stateroom and go over the maps and discuss what our objectives are and how we can obtain them with maximum results. Would you stop by around 2000 hours? You don't have to. This isn't an order. But we're going into your turf, Sergeant. I could use a little advice. This, I'm afraid, is my first time."

"I'll come over, sir. I'll see what I can do to help."

"Thank you, Sergeant. Thank you, men. Have a good evening and I'll see you all on the flight deck at 0700 tomorrow morning." The captain turned and walked out.

"Come on, Eddie, let's take a walk," Paul said. He laid the rifle on his cot and stood up, stretching to get the knots out of his muscles.

"Okay, pardner." Eddie was ahead of Paul and bounded to the door leading into the passageway.

They walked silently together through the maze of corridors until they came to the stern. They stood under the flight deck and watched the phosphorescent waters churning blue-green balls of color. The huge propellers were churning with a steady chopping motion and the wake seemed to be boiling out from the sea below.

Seaweed was tossed up with jellyfish. Steady glows of color appeared, beginning with light green and rolling into dark blue, spread out behind them like an evening sky.

"Paul, I'm getting real scared for you, bro. What are you going to do?"

"Jesus, Eddie, I don't know. Go eat their fuckin' chow. Go see the captain about their stupid fuckin' war games." Paul spat in the sea. "Fuck 'em. Fuck 'em all."

"Paul, we can't harm anyone or we're going against everything we believe in. Remember that poster we saw in the headshop in Jacksonville? Killing to end war is like balling to end love. That's straight scoop there, pardner, don't you think?"

"Yeah, Eddie, you're right. I think I am nuts, ya know?"

"You ain't nuts, pardner, you're angry and fed up. I can understand that. I get scary feelings thinking of you adding your name to that poem you wrote in 'Nam, but I respect the way you're fighting it. I like to think of you as a non-violent revolutionary. When I think of you pulling the trigger on a man, then I feel I don't know you, or that part of you, and I get real SCARED, man. Can you dig where I'm coming from?"

Paul turned and hugged Eddie.

"You're the only sane part of my life left," Paul said. "I feel real crazy in my head."

"It's not getting you, you don't have to let it get you."

"It doesn't get me, Eddie, it just takes me, ya know? Just takes me away with it." Paul was shaking his head as if he could no longer comprehend his own feelings. He shook his head because there was something racing around inside his mind that was almost always raging. He kept shaking his head because it seemed beyond his control. Some thin line had been stretched taut in the war in Vietnam, then had snapped somewhere in one of the battles, in one of the twenty-one combat operations he had taken part in. Now he could only see inside himself a feeling peering with blood-shot intent from his unconscious. Paul wanted it to go away but there was no language he could use to stop it. It understood no language. It surfaced anytime Paul was threatened. He tried to push it away by watching the sparkling jellyfish shoot up in quick-glowing green specks.

((Paul sat inside a small sandbagged bunker heating a can of ham-and-egg C-rations and boiling water for coffee. He was thinking of the night before when the NVA hit them. The enemy struck around 2 a.m. and they fought until dawn. He was wondering why the attackers hadn't come through the wire. Perhaps not a big enough force? The green tracer rounds thrashed in all through the night but from far outside the wire, from the treelines to the south and west. Paul and the men opened up with everything they had, M-16s and 14s, machine guns and 60 mm mortars. Perhaps they were pinpointing the location of the machine guns? Paul made a mental note to change the positions of the guns at dusk.

A marine's head bent over the reinforced fighting hole occupying the front opening of the bunker. It was Denny MacLean, a friend of Paul's from Eugene, Oregon who played the meanest game of cutthroat in the entire battalion. He swung his arm down inside the hole, gripping an M-14 with a selector switch that allowed you to fire full automatic, a badass weapon. Paul wished he had one.

"We gave em some last night! Puckered their assholes! Tightened em up, don't ya think?" Denny smiled at Paul with satisfaction.

Paul looked up from stirring his coffee.

"Well, maybe, Denny, maybe. But I gotta do some hard thinking today to get ready for tonight. I have a bad feeling about the way they're fighting us. A tough game of cutthroat."

"We didn't suffer a single casualty," Denny said, "plus we got to let off some steam, calm down a little, know what we can put out. Ya know what I'm sayin'?"

"Yeah, and that's what I'm worried about." Paul sipped his coffee. "What are you up to this morning?"

Another marine, small and skinny Gerry Jackson, jumped down and squatted in the bunker, smiling at Paul. Gerry was only eighteen but already had a wife and two children back home in Tennessee.

Gerry threw at Paul a pair of women's panties he was holding behind his back. Paul caught it, burying his face in it, then tossed it back to Gerry. Gerry's wife had sent him the black-laced lingerie soaked in perfume. All through the firefight the night before, Gerry and Denny ran from fighting hole to fighting hole with the green tracers streaking the mud at their feet, jumping in and pressing the panties into each marine's face like an oxygen mask. The marines would inhale deeply then fire like crazy. Paul smiled at the thought. He was thinking of writing them up for some kind of medal, but didn't know what it should be.

"So what are you *two* hooligans up to this morning?" Paul said, spooning some ham and eggs into his mouth.

"We're goin' outside the wire and gather some wood for our bunker. We wanna dig in and support it better."

"You both armed?"

"To the teeth!"

"Okay, I'll be out in a minute to cover you from up here, right after I eat."

"No sweat, Jose," Denny said, pulling his head and arm up as Gerry jumped out of the hole.

Paul leaned his M-16 next to him and continued his breakfast. He was trying to remember every detail of last night.

He recalled the first rounds coming in. Why so many tracers? Was the enemy merely taunting them? And not a single NVA tried to move in close.

BLAM!

Paul dropped his coffee into the fire and raced out, standing up in the hole and looking down at the wire. A puff of black smoke was lazily drifting from the ground. Paul could make out Gerry lying on his back. There was no doubt he was wounded.

"Contact! Outside the wire!" Paul screamed. "Everybody out!" He shouted as he climbed out of the hole and began running down the hill. Thinking only about the two fallen men, he had left his rifle behind.

It was thirty meters to the wire, then another twenty to where Gerry lay, all open terrain. He heard the pfffft of bullets slamming into the ground around him. He hurdled the wire and reached Gerry. A massive burst of firepower streamed out from the marines on top of the hill, zinging over his head like swift flying bees, stinging the trunks and branches of trees, pummeling the jungle.

Bending over Gerry, Paul saw small holes in the neck, all over the face and in the forehead. Gerry still clutched the panties in one hand.

"Corpsman!" Paul screamed. "Emergency medevac!" He saw the radio operator shouting into the handset. When he looked back, Gerry's eyes were staring at him. A large black fly landed on one of them and calmly walked across. Paul stood up and began to step back.

"Oh my God! Oh my God!" His next step had caused him to slip. He had stepped in something that resembled soft sausage and the slime of it almost made him fall. He was standing on intestines. The intestines were on the ground next to Denny. It was the first sight Paul had caught of Denny since the explosion.

Paul told at a glance what had probably happened. The gooks had tossed a grenade and Denny had tried to pick it up and throw it back. Denny's clothes had been blown off. He lay there nude and almost blending in with the ground. His arms were spread out like Christ's on the cross and both hands were blown away at the wrist. The explosion had somehow lifted everything up inside him, because where his belly should have been, there were his heart and lungs.

Paul's eyes widened. A fly landed on one of Denny's open eyes. He blinked. Denny's eyes moved slowly to Paul, focusing. Paul looked into them, seeing life.

Denny's mouth moved, not speaking but forming words that Paul understood. "Help me. Help me." Denny tried once more to form the words, then Paul saw Denny let go, saw the instant Denny's eyes glazed over.

Paul picked up Denny's M-14, now riddled with shrapnel holes in the stock and forearm, and emptied a magazine into the jungle, full automatic.

Doc Heinz had reached him by then. "Forget that one, he's dead!" He pulled Paul's sleeve toward Gerry. He ripped open Gerry's shirt and lifted his tee-shirt. Twenty or thirty small holes like the ones in his face and head covered his abdomen.

The corpsman motioned to Paul to press Gerry's chest. He bent over and gave Gerry mouth-to-mouth. Every time Doc blew in Paul pressed hard on Gerry's chest, three quick jerks. Each time Doc's mouth came away full of blood which he spat aside. Paul's hands became more and more soaked with the dark warm sticky fluid.

"It's no use, Paul, he's gone."

"Doc, I stepped in Denny's guts, he knew it! I know he knew it! And I couldn't do a thing, not a fucking thing to stop it!"

"Easy, Paul," Doc said, "this is the way the world ends out here."

After the medevac choppers carried Denny and Gerry away Paul went inside his bunker and began to punch the sandbags faster and faster until his knuckles bled.

Doc Heinz looked in on him. "How ya doin', Paul?" he asked quietly.

"I fucked up, Doc! I should have been outside covering them! I might have spotted the gooks. I could have saved them." Paul wiped his dirty forehead with a blood-soaked hand. The knuckles of both hands oozed blood that covered two precise spots on a sandbag. Doc shook his head sadly.

"Gerry and Denny the first men you've lost, Paul?"

"No, I lost my best friend in Hue City, I wasn't with him, but yes I was, I mean, I was with Gerry and Denny and I should have..."

"Shoulds are shit out here, Paul." Doc cut him off, duck-walked over to Paul and sat with his back against the sandbags. "What are you going to do with his rifle?" Doc asked.

"I'm gonna walk with it forever. I'm gonna carry it with me wherever I go. We're never gonna part!"

"Okay," Doc said, "there's gonna be more, Paul. That's what this thing is all about. Shooting people, blowing people up. They try to kill us, we try to kill them. It's all very simple so don't try to complicate it. There's gonna be more, Paul, maybe even you, you have to realize this and accept it or you're gonna go nuts. And I mean stark raving mad! I've seen it happen, especially to the ones with the responsibilities. I've seen 'em pushed to the point they blew their own heads off. Don't feel. Don't feel at all if you can help it. It'll suit you better, whether you go down or your buddies go down."

"Killing doesn't numb me, Doc, it makes me feel *more*! I still have my humanity. They can't take that!"

"Get off your high horse, fer chrissakes, Paul, look at the truth of the situation. Humanity and caring have no place in war. Just like killing has no place in peace. We all exist somewhere in the no-man's-land in between. The secret of this crazy life, I think, is to accept what the fuck you're facin' at all times. Do the best you can, that's all. Do the best you can."

Marines gathered outside the bunker, forming a circle around it, but nobody went in. They listened to the thudding and crying that resumed in the dark interior and waited silently.

It was war's equivalent of a church service, for all the men had their heads down as if they were praying, as if they, too, were part of the sobbing and angry punching that was their prayer, answering to one of the commandments of their being.

When the bunker got quiet they started breaking up, solemnly walking in twos and threes back to their own fighting holes to prepare for another night.))

"Paul, you're crying, you okay, pardner?" Eddie's voice cut across the abyss.

"I'll be okay, Eddie, thanks," Paul said, wiping his eyes.

"Let's take a hot shower and catch some chow, maybe then you'll feel better." Eddie would have made a hell of a corpsman, Paul thought.

He reached in his pocket and pulled out the three live bullets. Eddie looked at him. Paul smiled, then raised his fist like a left fielder making a play for homeplate, and threw the rounds as far as he could into the sea. The sea accepted them in silence.

"I'm really proud of you, Paul."

"No, don't be. Peace through fire superiority, ya know? I just decided those three rounds will never get the job done. The COM newsletter is where we have fire superiority. It's from there we'll make our final stand."

"I'm with you to the end, you know that," Eddie said with total sincerity.

They made their way to their quarters through the complicated interior of the ship. They took hot showers, ate and returned. Eddie was going to the movie while Paul went to the captain's quarters.

Paul looked in the mirror as he got ready to leave. He saw fatigue, but the burning anger was gone.

He knocked three times on the captain's door. It felt like boot camp again.

"Come in," Captain Pelham said.

"Sergeant Timons reporting as ordered, sir." Paul saluted.

"I didn't order you, Sergeant," said the captain, returning the salute. "Please sit down, Sergeant."

Paul took a seat and glanced quickly around. How much more luxury the officers had. A brown chaise longue spread across one corner of the room where portholes let in the cool salt breeze. The two beds had thick mattresses. The captain sat behind a small fold-up desk. Paul noticed shiny brass fittings and a blue-grey coat of paint on the bulkheads which was soft on his eyes.

"How can I help you, sir?" he volunteered.

"Your field experience is very important in a small unit like ours. I'm learning. I've always wanted a field commission, you know, and now that I have one I want our unit to be tight, accurate, and put on a good show for the brass."

"Good show, yes, I understand, sir."

Captain Pelham looked at Paul. How was it that this sergeant always pulled out exactly the statement he wanted from every remark of his? This irritated him but intrigued him, too.

"What do you mean by that, Sergeant Timons?"

"Well, sir, like I said to you in the troop quarters, that's all this rinky-dink operation is, a good show."

"We can only practice war, simulate it as best we can. We can't have bodies scattered out there in the swamps, now, can we? If we allowed that, no one would make it to the war."

"Exactly, sir."

"You're a hard nut, Timons. What can I or the Marine Corps say that you won't take wrong?"

"Nothing now, sir. I know too much."

"Maybe you don't know as much as you think. You may not know that Staff Sergeant Harris wants your ass out of the unit. He wants you transferred. He wishes he could send you back to 'Nam."

"I know that too, sir. But with only four months left, I don't think he can pull it off." Paul smiled.

"Listen, Sergeant, before we get down to business there's something I must tell you. Harris believes you are a communist subversive involved in anti-war activities at the camp. He told me he saw proof in writing that you are involved. Is this true?"

"The war must stop."

"The best way to stop the war is to win it, don't you think?"

"Begging the captain's pardon, sir, but we can't win. We're losing it everywhere. In the paddies, in the mountains, thousands of us are dying and we are losing. The American government is fucking with all of us. They wanna cover our bodies with American flags. They wanna bury us all. If you get shipped overseas you'll find this out very quickly. The Vietnamese people hate us, the American people hate us, the North Vietnamese hate us, the Vietcong hate us. Shit, Captain, the rich are well enough off to keep out of it. But those rich boys badmouth *us*, the ones fighting and bleeding and dying. For their ideals, sir? I think not." Paul looked searchingly at the captain.

Pelham was trying to think of a clear answer, but his mind was swimming in a morass of misconceptions and evil truths he could not put into words. This sergeant was the one man who could do this to him.

"Shit, Sergeant," Pelham said with force, "I can't answer the goddamn question. I only get more pissed thinking about it."

"Now you're becoming a field marine, a grunt. Now you're learning, sir." Paul beamed at the officer.

"I get so fucking mad." Pelham raised his arm. "I get so fucking angry I could smash my fist into something. Only I don't know where or what to smash the damn thing into."

"Yessir, yessir," Paul said approvingly.

"Maybe that's why Harris is after your butt. Maybe he feels this weird anger and this is his home, his beloved Corps, like mine, and he's ready to explode." Paul looked at him with sympathetic eyes. Pelham felt he had finally said something that made sense to Timons.

"Sir, I think now you are beginning to understand."

"I don't know, Sergeant."

"Listen, sir, I want to help you with this rinky-dink operation, or whatever you call it, because now I know that you know." Paul peered at the officer and Pelham saw what he thought were strange narrow eyes cracking with fiery intensity like a rifle range. The captain did not know that Paul was accepting him as a brother. Instead, he felt an unfamiliar fear rise inside him. It started in his heart the moment he looked at Paul's eyes, then climbed to his throat and raced to his temples, grabbing them so tight he felt a throbbing from which he thought he would faint. Paul gave him a wide-eyed smile.

"I feel very happy, sir, that you know."

"I'd like to talk to you more about this another time, but we have to get down to business." Pelham picked up a two-foot square map from the floor and placed it on his desk. It represented the coastline just south of Swansboro, North Carolina. The map encompassed about ten square miles broken down into grid squares each a kilometer wide. The officer pointed his finger at a bracketed section where each klick was marked. Though small, it was an extremely swampy area a kilometer in from the beach.

"This is where the team is going in tomorrow."

"How they taking us in?"

"Helicopters."

"I'd rather go in on airboats."

"Why?"

"Because suppose the swamp and marsh are up to our necks. The chopper hovers, we jump and bango we're fucked." Paul looked up.

"I've already covered that, Sergeant," Pelham said proudly.

"What do you mean, sir?"

"When we arrived today I sent a small observation helicopter to recon the area and he found a field of solid ground about 300 by 600 feet. The pilot said the field was surrounded by trees, which means good cover until you can get your bearings. It's also less than 600 meters from where you'll implant the devices, so you don't hump far. You get the job done. I insert you safely and I bring you out safely." Very pleased with himself, Pelham followed by delivering his last thought to Paul. "You're not spending the night out there. I believe this will take only about three hours, then I'm having you extracted and brought back to the ship. On this one, at least I can bring you back quickly and give you hot chow, a shower and a movie. What do you think, Sergeant?"

"I think, sir, you don't need my advice at all. I think you're a good commanding officer and I'm proud to serve under you. I don't say that to many officers."

"I'll be operating out of S-2 and COC aboard this ship. Tomorrow morning you will head a team with nine other men, right here." The captain pointed to the map. "You'll implant three devices within fifty feet of each other and shoot eight-digit coordinates. Then I'll pull you out. Day after tomorrow you go back in, recover the devices and by airboat implant them in a new location. Your call-sign will be Hungarian and ours Seaworthy. Here's your shackle code for the radio frequencies we'll be operating on. You'll get through this one fine, I believe."

Pelham tried to imagine a real combat situation. Here he was telling his sergeant, an experienced pointman, where he would have to go to encounter the enemy. He felt odd with power. He realized the courage it took for an enlisted man to take an order in the face of imminent combat or death. Timons knew all the odds. Pelham wondered how many times he had stood in front of his CO's desk at 3rd Recon in Quang-Tri receiving this same kind of order. He felt a deep respect for Paul.

"No problem, sir," Paul replied. "Do you want me to arm them?"

"Yes, arm them just like the real thing. You can disarm them easily, don't you think?"

"Well, sir, that depends. Overseas we armed them when we implanted them and that was it. They had a four-month lifespan, then automatically self-destructed. If the mud and silt shift them more than four degrees off center they'll self-destruct before we can get to them. We'll have to be very careful digging them up in mud. But perhaps it will work. I have my doubts, but we'll see."

"That's exactly what we want to find out on this exercise."

"Well, I don't like staying on ships too long anyway. I'll go prepare the men and gear, square everything away. Be talkin' with you on the radio next time, sir." Paul stood up to leave.

"You're not a subversive, are you, Sergeant?"

"I'm sure as hell not a communist. I fought and killed them for a living. The Marine Corps trained me and sent me. I believe everything I do from here on out is a fight for freedom. I never felt that in Vietnam. Here in America I feel it very strongly."

"You don't have to say anything more, Sergeant. Good luck."

Paul and the captain exchanged salutes, then shook hands. Paul left Pelham staring out the porthole, watching the evening slip from sight in the west while the heavier darkness in the east rose across sky and ocean with an ominous spreading density that seemed to pull all of night over the officer's soul.

In the ship's hold, after the movie, Paul assembled his team. He patiently explained what was going to take place.

"Above all, listen to me," he said. He looked especially closely at Eddie. "Stay together but don't bunch up. Keep the man in front in sight at all times and be aware of who's behind you."

"I'll walk tail-end charlie," Eddie said, trying to be helpful.

"No, Eddie, I'm walking point and you're secondary point. Lance Corporal Johnson will walk tail-end charlie with the backup radio. You're fresh out of radio school in San Diego, aren't you, Johnson?"

"Yes, Sergeant. I graduated last month, they promoted me and I thought I'd have my orders for 'Nam. But instead I got leave and orders to the 2nd Marines. Disappointed me, but what can I say? I have to make the best of it."

"They probably saved your ass. Be thankful of that and don't rush going to 'Nam. That little fucker is going to be there for a long time." Paul placed a gentle hand on Johnson's arm. "Keep the handset pressed to your ear and listen to how I handle the transmissions. Just follow us, listen and learn. That's all you have to do."

"Yes, Sergeant."

"Okay, men, let's hit the racks. Tomorrow we get to exercise for these fuckers. This one belongs to them, not us. Let's get through it and race back to Jacksonville and the slop-chutes. Any other questions?"

The men looked sleepily at Paul. He smiled to himself when he said goodnight to them. Here in training they could sleep. In war you did not sleep, you catnapped. You learned to hump long distances under the harshest conditions without sleep. Fuck sleep. It was nectar, the drink of the gods not of the warrior. Tonight they could be gods. Tomorrow perhaps they would learn something about what comprised their existence in the heat of these dangerous times, and about who made the decisions on what it was that gods turned warriors turned mortal men might ultimately become.

Paul smoked a last cigarette in the darkness, listening to the men cough and snore. Then he lay down and waited for his hard restless sleep. It would be a sleep full of enemy soldiers with red eyes and spiked bayonets lunging for his throat. They assaulted him every night.

He tried to think of beautiful Carla. Though he never made love to her while he knew her, he saw his nude body warming against her soft, smooth flesh. He imagined his hand caressing her sleek calf muscles, touching the small hairs of her thighs. His hand moved closer to the sweet opening of her womanhood that he so feverishly wanted to enter, to make love with all his manly being, to penetrate her with his strength and gentleness. When sleep took Paul the opening of her body was transformed into a fighting hole that completely swallowed him like a grave.

The early-rising eastern sun greeted them on the flight deck the following morning along with the whining and revving of helicopter engines and navy and marines doing what they do best. Playing war. Paul sat against his rucksack, a radio stuck under the flap, a three-foot tape antenna protruding from the top. He listened to the crackling transmissions and waited for the bird that would take them in. He could no longer count the number of times he had done this. He let himself appear to be the laziest do-nothing marine out there. Eddie shouted over the heat and blast of the chopper engines.

"Well, we're finally going on a patrol together and I'll be right behind you. I'll be watching your back." Eddie smiled.

"Yeah, thanks, pardner, you watch my back. But keep the closest eye on your own ass. Stay twenty meters behind me but keep me in sight. If I trip a mine, catch a sniper's bullet or spring an ambush, forget me. Get the other men organized and get them out. If something happens to me you're second in command. Get the radio if you can. If I'm down and silent and you're trapped, just empty a magazine of ammo into me and my pack and radio. Then get the hell out of there and call in artillery and gunship support. Got it?" Paul was serious.

"All we got is blanks for our rifles, Paul."

"This is an exercise for war. That's how I'm teaching you. This is our first patrol together. Listen to everything I tell you."

"Even if this was for real I'd never leave you out there. We wouldn't move till we got you."

Paul stuck his index finger under Eddie's throat and lifted it with force, pressing it up against his chin.

"This is war. Don't fuck with me, Eddie, when I tell you something. What I say goes out there. Whatever you do, keep as many men alive as you can. They drop me, you do as I've told. If they get me make sure I'm wasted, then leave me. Throw a frag, for chrissakes, but get yourself and the other men out of there. No questions, you boot fuck."

Eddie began to see what combat was. If this were a real patrol, there'd be a good chance Paul would not come back, or perhaps any of them if the team leader didn't sense the dangers they were walking into. Eddie saw a serenity in Paul's eyes that came from being as salty as Paul was. He knew that Paul was going into his field of life, the only place where he understood the rules.

In the helicopter Paul's anger lifted and stared around with intent eyes, then lay back. They were going home again.

The chopper cleared the flight deck and circled the ship, then its nose dipped and raced toward the mainland. It gathered speed and altitude then leveled off at fifteen hundred feet. Paul watched out the window at the bristling blue ocean where he could see large fish, perhaps whales or huge sharks, swinging their tails in hypnotic motion. Two of them moved away from a lone animal while several others circled. Paul kept watching the motion of the tails.

((Paul's recon team was circling four klicks northeast of the Rockpile. They were in a smaller helicopter, a UH-1, called a slick. The slicks took them into combat patrols. Paul saw himself sitting in the open bay door just behind the pilot, in front of the door gunner. He sat next to his best friend, Nicky Martinez, their legs dangling out the side and caught by the breeze blowing with force toward the tail.

They hung on for dear life, Paul and Nicky on one side, Doc Heinz and Fred Garvey on the other, and between them two men whom Paul could not recognize. They leaned back on their loaded rucksacks for support. Paul carried ten grenades and wondered if he should have carried more ammunition. He never felt he had enough.

Suddenly they were descending, the chopper's tail snapping back and forth like the great fish of the sea. Paul watched the jungle coming up like an immersed dark hunt for death, full of horror and darker secrets. He flipped his rifle to full automatic. He held his index finger near the trigger, gripping the stock tighter and sliding his other hand past the magazine and bolt, clenching the smooth wood that covered and cooled the barrel.

They were going in on a ridge that appeared to be at least eight hundred meters high, the whole ridge overlooking the expanse of valley below. At twelve hundred feet and descending, Paul's heart started pounding, he took on the dizzy detachment of a man entering combat. His face was a green and black camouflaged grimace.

The air darkened for a moment and Paul heard a loud chopping crash beneath them. The slick shuddered like a death gasp as something pounded into the bottom of it.

An explosion erupted underneath them, they were stunned.

The eruption was a fireball, the heat blasting through the interior of the slick. Paul heard the whizzing of metal as the fireball singed his hair. Hot hydraulic fluid spurted from holes in the chopper, hitting his face mixed with the warm blood of the wounded.

The shadow beneath them came out. A CH-46 helicopter appeared below and to the right with only its front rotor blade gasping for air. The rear rotor blade had struck the slick and the main engine had exploded. Paul caught sight of the co-pilot for a second. The visored face was like a smashed beetle which peered intently for the last time at what struck him from the air.

They veered away from each other, the larger craft dropping like a rock, the slick auto-rotating with great force. They were going to crash.

The slick's pilot fought the controls and jerked his feet on the foot rudders, fighting the rapid descent. They shook hard right and left like a big hand slapping a face. The earth met them. They hit hard on the side of a hill well below the ridge they were orginally to go in on.

Paul was ejected, his body punched into the ground, rolling uncontrollably, his rifle flying out of his hands, pack and suspender straps torn from his body. He finally stopped face down and could hear only a loud throbbing in his head. Black smoke billowed from the large craft that was burning out of control about three hundred meters away. Paul smelled the burning flesh.

He was up and running to the slick. He dragged away from it a wounded gunner sliced open by a huge chunk of rotor blade. A door-gunner, his left arm limp and dripping blood, ran to the craft and began to haul radio equipment out of the cockpit.

The sky around them seemed to fill with aircraft as the mayday flew through the frequencies of the other pilots' headsets. Nicky looked at Paul, his eyes wide. In his South Bronx accent he said "Paul Timons, what a horror. Paul Timons, what a horror. Paul Timons, what a horror. Paul Timons...")

They passed the coastline and Paul saw hundreds of marines looking up at them from the beach. They descended past muddy swamps and little inlets of water. Paul's heart froze. They were going to crash!

Instead, he saw trees, towering North Carolina pines. They surrounded a small mounded field that was dry and well above the water line. The helicopter braked hard and he felt a sharp jerk when the wheels touched down.

The rear loading ramp dropped and Paul and the team raced out. The tall grass and weeds were blown back flat against the rush of air from the rotors.

Paul ran toward the front of the craft. Shielding his face against the blast of air he waited until the team cleared the chopper, then gave a thumbs-up to the door-gunner who signaled the pilot on his headset. The pilot glanced at Paul, his visored beetle face impassive. Then the chopper roared off the ground and gained altitude.

Paul was on the handset.

"Seaworthy, Seaworthy, this is Hungarian, over."

"Hungarian, Seaworthy," the captain's voice came crackling

over the radio.

"Roger, Seaworthy, this is Hungarian, I have you five by, how me, over."

"Hungarian, Seaworthy. I have you five by."

"Seaworthy, Hungarian, we are at papa-kilo-sierra. I bracket, niner-sixer-zero, fiver-two-four. How copy, over."

"Roger, Hungarian, I copy, papa-kilo-sierra, niner-sixer-zero, fiver-two-four, over."

"Roger, Seaworthy, you have a solid. We're moving out, over."

"Roger, Hungarian."

Paul stood up and watched the compass needle settle. He laid the map on the ground and oriented it with the compass. Then he looked off in the distance where they would be moving.

"Let's go, men."

He felt a rush inside him. Something about walking point always terrified but exhilarated Paul.

The thicker scrub pines and brush scraped at his legs as he entered the marshy area of the implant site. He swung his rifle barrel so it always looked where he looked. Mud began to suck at his ankles and pull him down. But the more the terrain tried to hinder his progress the more he set his jaw and tightened his thigh muscles and pushed on.

Paul had the handset clipped to his suspender straps and could hear the transmissions being sent by other units operating in the area. He moved three hundred meters out from the treeline and found the mud now sucking at calf height. Five hundred meters out and he was sinking to his knees, having to lift with great force to pull each leg free and take the next step. The sun burned down on them as it reached toward its zenith. The men were soaked in sweat and were attacked on their faces and hands by black horseflies and swarms of mosquitoes.

"Seaworthy, Seaworthy, Hungarian, over."

"Hungarian, Seaworthy, go." Paul recognized Pelham's voice coming from shipboard. He knew that the captain was in a fresh uniform, probably sipping coffee, leaning back in his chair smoking a cigarette and enjoying his field command.

"Seaworthy, Hungarian. The going is rough. We are in the open and making slow progress, over."

"Roger, I copy, Hungarian. Keep with it. How close to implant, over."

"Seaworthy, Hungarian. Within one hundred meters, over."

"Roger, Hungarian. Pick your spot, keep with it, over."

Keep with it? Paul's camouflaged face dripped sweat as he turned and looked at the team. War games? He saw nine men in the open and waited for the sniper's rifle to crack the silence. What the fuck was he doing? He raised his hand and halted the team. He motioned them to squat.

When they did so the mud and water soaked their crotches and they became more miserable. Paul pulled the map from his breast pocket and orientated it with the compass. He could barely make out the treeline where they had been brought in. Everything else was open marsh and swamp, no tree or brush higher than three feet.

"Eddie, come up here," Paul whispered.

Eddie slogged up to Paul with difficulty, holding his rifle free with one hand, using the other to lift each leg, then place it down in the deepening mud. He made loud noises. "Yo, pardner, what's up?" Eddie said.

"See over there to the left of the scrub pine? Looks like a little high ground. That's where we'll implant their devices, dig?"

"Yeah, bro, is that where they want them?"

"Close enough for government use, don't ya think?"

"You're the boss, Paul. Do you think I could walk point going back?"

"No way, Jose. What if you stumble into a sinkhole or something? Then I gotta haul your ass out." Paul was squinting at Eddie. "Besides, I never walk behind anyone out here. Do you understand, bro?"

"Yeah, I do, Paul." Eddie was looking around in a very professional manner, searching for the enemy.

"Save your eyes," Paul advised him. "If this was injun country we'da been dead as soon as we came out of that treeline."

"Well, what the fuck, man. How the hell do you survive in 'Nam?"

"You fight your ass off, simple as that."

"What if this were 'Nam, Paul? What would you do?"

"It would be suicide and I would have aborted the mission before we touched down."

"But what about orders?"

"I try to keep men alive," Paul said. "The fuckin' generals really don't have the slightest iota of what we have to go through. I would take a court martial before I'd walk you guys out in the open like this. But the captain told me he reconned this place and it would be easy. Fat chance."

"He tried to do his best for us, Paul. We can't blame him."

"Well, I want to blame someone, goddamn it. Someone is an absolute idiot. They're trying to kill us. The training and even 'Nam was for them. To learn. We'll just get this the fuck over with and get out. Pass what I told you back to the other men. Let them pass it one at a time so each man knows. Go." Paul looked ahead at the mound.

"Wish we had a joint or some JD out here. I could use a hit and a snort," Eddie said.

"Yeah, then we're stoned and drunk and we'd be sloshing around here for a week. You bring any Hendrix tapes?" Paul grinned.

"Purple Haze, all in my brain/lately things, they don't mean the same/actin' funny, but I don't know why/'scuse me while I kiss the sky," Eddie sang. Then he was up and lifting his legs to pass the word to the other men.

Paul traversed the hundred meters to the mound, which was about twenty by forty feet and packed hard. Paul ordered the men to form a circle. He pulled out the map and compass for final calculations.

"This is just crazy, man, I'm losing it. This is ridiculous."

"Hang in there, we're halfway done," Eddie said.

"How are the men holding up? Go around and check. See if they're okay. See if anyone is sick or dizzy from the heat. Then get right back to me." Eddie nodded and moved among the men.

"Seaworthy, Seaworthy, Hungarian, over."

"Hungarian, Seaworthy, go."

"This is Hungarian. Can we get any spotter rounds out here?"

"Negative on your last, Hungarian. No arty fire. That's the

American mainland you're on." In the shipboard command center Captain Pelham was scrunching up his face and wondering what Timons was up to.

"Seaworthy, Hungarian. How the fuck am I going to get a proper azimuth without a spotter round? No prominent landmarks except our LZ, over."

"Hungarian, Seaworthy. Watch your language on this net. Shoot a coordinate from the LZ and cross it on your line of detention, over." Pelham was feeling frustrated.

"Yeah, right, Seaworthy. You want eight-digit coordinates? I'll give you six and hope we're close, over."

"Hungarian, Seaworthy. Eight-digit. That's an order, over."

"Yeah, Seaworthy. What you think I am, an Einstein? Over."

"Hungarian, keep to proper radio protocol. You're the pro. I know you can do it."

"Yeah, Seaworthy, I can do it. Just like Custer did it, over."

On a hundred handsets scattered about the units on the beach and among those beginning to make their way inland on airboat, laughter broke out.

"Hungarian, Seaworthy. Follow orders, I repeat, follow orders, over."

"Well, now, let me think about this for a while, over."

"Hungarian, Seaworthy. You can do it, over."

"Seaworthy, I only got you one by. I have to switch batteries, over."

On the Guam Pelham threw the handset down in disgust and began running his fingers through his hair and pacing up and down among the officers and men hooked to their units. The other officers watched Pelham closely but said nothing. They were waiting to see how he would handle it. He was all alone. The battalion commander, a lieutenant colonel, approached him.

"I want to know the name of that man, Captain." His square face shone over four rows of ribbons.

"Sir," Pelham began, "the man is my best. He's a vet of a lot of combat. His service record book shows twenty-one major combat operations. He has a Letter of Commendation and Purple Heart and other decorations. He's capable. Salty, I'll agree, sir. But, sir, I can handle him."

"What's his name?" the battalion commander insisted.

"Sergeant Paul Timons, sir."

The colonel wrote the name in his pocket notebook and looked sternly at Pelham. "I want him disciplined, do you understand, Captain? Salty don't get it in this man's Marine Corps. Not with a buck sergeant. Understand, Captain?" Then he added, "Do I make my point perfectly clear?"

"Yes, sir," Pelham said loudly, "I'll handle it, sir." He felt his precious field command slipping away and maybe even his beloved twin captain's bars. He was furious with Paul. He had tried to make the patrol as easy as possible and, as usual, it did not suit Timons. He picked up the handset.

"Hungarian, Hungarian, this is Seaworthy, over." No reply. He repeated it. Still no reply.

On the hot marshy mound Paul had heard the captain's transmissions clearly, he had Pelham five by on the radio and didn't need to switch batteries. He was tired of talking.

Paul looked around for anything on the map he could shoot reference on for something as fine as eight-digit coordinates. There was nothing. No prominent landmarks at all. No hills, no distinct streams or rivers. Nothing. Only the landing zone in the grove of trees. And that was over six hundred meters behind them.

"What the fuck, over. What the fuck, over," Paul said out loud.

Eddie returned. "The men are holding up fine, Paul. They all have complete trust in you."

"Yeah, yeah, everyone has complete trust in me but them." He pointed his finger straight up at the sky. "They won't listen to shit I got to say."

"Easy, bro, you'll get it," Eddie said reassuringly.

"I'm going to get it alright." He looked around. "You guys dig out the devices and get them ready. Attach the antennas and stand by. I have the arming key."

"Okay, Paul, relax," Eddie said. He moved back to the other men who remained silent and seemed in awe of the brash buck sergeant.

Paul decided to go by instinct. He guessed the approximate distance and the azimuth they had traversed. He shackled together an eight-digit coordinate he thought might be close. This will jar them, he thought.

"Seaworthy, Seaworthy, Hungarian. Back on line, how read, over."

"Hungarian, Seaworthy. I have you five by, how me, over." Pelham was aware his hands were sweating as he gripped the handset.

"Roger, Seaworthy, Hungarian. I have you five by. Stand by for coordinate implant, over."

"Hungarian, Seaworthy, standing by, over." Captain Pelham felt relief.

"Seaworthy, Hungarian. Ready to copy, over."

"Hungarian, Seaworthy. Ready, over."

"Christ," Paul said in an aside, "I'm gonna lose my voice talkin' all the time to these idiots. I tell you it wears me out." The men laughed.

"Seaworthy, Hungarian. I shackle papa, sierra, tango, charlie. November, oscar, tango, tango. How copy, over." Paul widened his eyes to the team, puffed up his cheeks and let out his breath.

"Hungarian, Seaworthy. I copy papa, sierra, tango, charlie. November, oscar, tango, tango, over."

"Roger, Seaworthy, you have a solid. Stand by. We will implant, over."

"Roger, Hungarian, standing by, over." Pelham lit a cigarette and took a long swallow of coffee. He looked at the battalion commander. The colonel smiled and nodded his head in approval.

On the hard-packed mound Paul had the men dig three holes about fifteen feet apart big enough to bury a shoe-box size device. He lowered the seismic sensors one by one into the holes, always checking to see that the level's bubble was dead center. He packed wet mud against the sides to hold the instruments steady. Then he inserted the T-shaped arming key into the first mechanism and locked it, then did the same to the other two.

"Cover them over carefully, men. Realize that if you shake or move them more than four degrees off center they'll self-destruct. If you should move them, get your hands free. They don't explode but they burn like hell, enough to blister your hands. Got it?"

The men nodded and began packing mud so the instruments were covered except for an eight-inch antenna sticking out the top.

Suddenly one of the new men slipped and hit the edge of one of the devices so it was kicked off center. It started to burn with an internal searing noise. The young marine pulled his hands free and the sensor burned out with intensity.

"Oh, shit, Sergeant Timons, I blew it," the young marine said with desperation.

"Are you okay? Let me see your hands. You didn't get burned, did you?"

"No, Sergeant," the embarrassed young marine replied.

"Well, long as you're okay. Not much else we can do," Paul said. "We need a string of three devices, two won't hack it. This mission failed and it serves the bastards right. Too damp, too muddy. Don't worry, Private, you were doing your best. You're learning. It takes time and practice, so be cool, okay?"

"Yes, Sergeant."

Paul went back on the handset.

"Seaworthy, Hungarian, over."

"Hungarian, Seaworthy, go."

"Seaworthy, Hungarian. One sierra-india-delta self-destructed. Two in, over."

"Shit!" Pelham exclaimed. The battalion commander was staring at him.

"Hungarian, Seaworthy, over."

"Seaworthy, Hungarian," Paul replied wearily.

"This is Seaworthy. Leave the two implanted and make your way back to the LZ. Once back, relay and I'll have a bird come get you, over."

"Roger your last, Seaworthy. Returning to LZ. Will relay for extraction as soon as we are there, over."

The battalion commander was fuming. He stalked from his chair overlooking the maps and radios and went straight for Pelham.

"Captain Pelham, there will be no chopper sent for those men. They failed. It's about fifteen hundred meters to the beach. Have the team march. A good walk may well set their heads straight for the next time."

"Is that an order, sir? I'd rather get my men out quickly. That's the nature of our operation." Pelham realized right away he had said the wrong thing.

"Don't question me, Captain, ever, do you understand?"

"Yes, sir." Pelham's stomach sank to his groin. He picked up the handset again.

"Hungarian, Seaworthy, over."

"Hungarian, go." Paul waited for the news.

"Hungarian, Seaworthy. No chopper available now. The beach is fifteen hundred meters due east. Make your way to it, over."

"This is Hungarian. That's too long a haul with the amount of gear we're carrying. Suggest overnight at LZ for extraction in the morning, over." Paul let out a deep breath.

"Negative, Hungarian. Follow the order, over." Pelham felt awful after having promised to get them out quickly and he knew what lay ahead of them.

"Seaworthy, Hungarian. May I suggest an airboat for extraction, over." Paul placed his hand on his forehead and rubbed hard.

Pelham looked over at the battalion commander. The colonel rushed over to Pelham and snatched the handset from his hand.

"Hungarian, this is Seaworthy, over."

"Seaworthy, Hungarian, go. Over."

"Hungarian, this is Oscar-5 Tango. You will do as ordered. No questions. No suggestions. Do it. Do you understand? Over."

"Yeah, bro, I understand. You're gonna fuck us in the ass because a private made a private's mistake, over." Paul looked at the team, face by face. They were all wide-eyed.

"Hungarian, Seaworthy. I'll see you personally when you return to this ship, over."

"Yeah, this is Hungarian. My pleasure, I'm sure."

Paul could go no further. He was done with them. They could do what they wanted with him. He'd rather be a private anyway. Paul hung the handset on his suspenders and pulled his ruck to his shoulders. The other men copied him. "We're fucked, as usual," he said.

Paul led them out. The going was rough and got steadily worse. It took four hours of tough humping to make a thousand meters through extremely thick mud. Though Paul led them on an erratic course to avoid what he believed was the worst of the swamp, the mud, covered by a thin layer of water, was now up to their thighs. They could barely move. Paul looked back at the nine men.

"Tighten it up to ten feet apart," he yelled. He counted the men. He counted eight. He counted again.

"Eddie, we're short a man!" Paul gasped, adrenalin rushing through him.

"Holy shit!" Eddie shouted, counting also. "Tail-end charlie's gone. Johnson with the secondary radio."

Paul grabbed the handset, keyed it and screamed "Johnson, Johnson, can you read me, over." Paul struck his forehead with his fist. "Johnson, Johnson, can you hear me, bro, answer, answer, over."

Pelham immediately came up on the net.

"Hungarian, Seaworthy. What's going on, over."

"Seaworthy, we're short a man and stranded. Can't move. Mud up to our thighs and getting deeper. Send an airboat. Send a bunch of airboats. And helicopters, for chrissakes, over."

In the command center the battalion commander stood up to monitor what was happening. Pelham looked at him with pleading eyes.

"They're missing a man and bogged down in heavy swamp. It's starting to get late and with night we don't stand a chance of finding the lost man. What should we do, sir?"

"Tell him we'll send two airboats right away and I'll dispatch a chopper to look for the lost man." The battalion commander's voice was now filled with concern.

"Hungarian, Seaworthy. Stay where you are. We're sending two airboats. One to pick you up and one to search for Johnson. A chopper will also be on the scene for the rescue. What is your location, over." Pelham felt nauseous.

"How the fuck do I know where we are? Stuck in mud up to our waists. Can't move."

"Hang in there, Hungarian. We'll have the chopper find you

and the airboats will get you out. We'll find Johnson, over." Pelham wanted to cry.

"What the fuck. You punish us. Now you want to save us. What in hell is going on here, over."

"Be calm, Hungarian. Be calm. We're on our way, over."

The men stood still, up to their waists in muddy water, scared and exhausted. They were eight statues, they didn't move at all. They had found trying to move only caused them to sink deeper into a slow quicksand.

Somewhere behind them in the thickness of the swamp of snakes and blackflies and mosquitoes there was a marine. Perhaps stuck and unable to call out. Perhaps with a dead radio. Paul hoped and prayed. He began to cry. "Oh please, God. I've lost so many men, protect and watch over Johnson until we can rescue him. Oh please, God!" They waited.

Within twenty minutes a chopper appeared in the distance. Paul watched the approaching speck gather form and grabbed the handset.

"Seabreeze, Seabreeze, Hungarian, over."

The voice that came up on the net was urgent and spoke over the whine of rotor engines.

"Hungarian, Seabreeze, over."

"Seabreeze, Hungarian." Paul watched the chopper as it snorted through the air just north of them. "Be advised you are north of us. We are at your nine o'clock, over."

Paul watched as the chopper's nose changed direction and the bird headed toward them dropping to five hundred feet. He was back on the handset.

"Seabreeze, Hungarian. We are at your twelve o'clock. Dead on. Do you want a smoke? Over." Paul was preparing to pull the pin on a green smoke grenade. The helicopter was almost directly above them.

"Hungarian, Seabreeze. Negative on the smoke. We have you in sight, over."

The helicopter dropped straight down rapidly until it hovered just overhead and its shadow was a windy pall over the men. Paul heard the pilot on the radio giving coordinates to the airboat crews, then back to him.

"This is Seabreeze. In what direction have you been moving? Over."

"Due east for the last one thousand meters, over."

"Roger, Hungarian. Hang on, men, the boats are coming. Over."

The chopper roared off in search of Johnson. The men were silent. Unable to lift their legs, they stood like objects fixed in cement, except for their eyes, which were anxiously pinned on Paul. All their hopes rested on him.

"Be easy, men. They're coming, they're coming."

Paul peered to the east through his binoculars. He saw the bows of two airboats just above the mud and water line speeding toward them across the stink grasses, skimming over the surface of the swamp.

"Here they come!" Paul shouted.

In a matter of minutes marines reached with strong hands and pulled the men from the mud, making deep sloshing noises.

The men were all helped to one boat. They lay on the deck too exhausted to move or take off any of their gear. The other boat flew inland whirring its fan blades.

There was radio contact with the chopper that had flown east in search of Johnson. Paul lay back against his rucksack and listened to the transmissions. The helicopter had spotted him. Paul could see the craft hovering over a spot about eight hundred meters behind them. A corpsman was making his way carefully down the swinging steps of a rope ladder.

"Noride, Seabreeze, over."

"Seabreeze, Noride."

"You have us in eye contact, over."

"Roger, Seabreeze. Eye contact and closing, over."

The voice of the staff sergeant in charge of the airboat was clouding the net. Other units remained quiet as they listened to the rescue effort. Paul's eyes choked with tears. The airboat raced down the inlet to the wide expanse of the Atlantic. The other one was now directly under the chopper. They were pulling a limp body out of the muddy water.

"Seaworthy, Noride, over."

"Noride, Seaworthy, go." There was great pain in Captain Pelham's voice, which seemed to come from a great distance.

"We have a dead marine out here." The sergeant's voice was breaking as he relayed the grim information. "Appears to have drowned. Found face down in the water. Weight of his gear must have pushed him down and he couldn't get up. Probably had no chance to cry out or signal distress, over."

Captain Pelham and the battalion commander stood rigid at their posts. The marines manning the radios were silent, their eyes cast down. Captain Pelham dropped the handset and turned to his commander.

"Sir, may I be excused from my post at this time?" He kept his eyes averted from the colonel. He was dizzy and afraid of falling.

"Yes, Captain, get some air. I'll have a chopper bring your men in from the beach. I want to talk to the sergeant in charge as soon as they are back on board." He breathed deeply and coughed to clear his lungs.

"Aye, aye, sir," Pelham said, saluting without making eye contact. The colonel quickly returned the salute and went back to his command post. The captain walked at a brisk pace to the rail of the ship. Sweat poured from him as the waves of the Atlantic below lapped against the ship with a gentle sound.

Events moved fast for the team being ferried by the airboat. The inlet to the ocean seemed to shrink from a large artery to a small vein and then the boat stopped. The team disembarked and trudged down the white sandy beach past other marines digging in. They watched the exhausted men walk by in single file, the camouflage paint streaking off their faces with sweat, their utilities sticking to their bodies.

"Go easy, bros." None of the team members answered. They followed Paul whose face was a mask behind which razor teeth were grinding, ready to sink into something.

At the beach edge, where white-capped waves broke over the sand, a chopper came at them low over the ocean. The nose pulled up, the rear wheels settled, the front wheel stayed off the ground as the craft hovered. The rear loading ramp opened like a dark mouth and swallowed the team into its interior. The ramp closed as the big bird gained altitude and sped back to the Guam.

Once on the flight deck the men hurried off to their quarters in single file. The last red rays of the setting sun spread like a carpet over their staring eyes.

Paul removed his gear and dropped the wet mess on the floor. He threw his muddy rifle on top of the pile. His eyes had changed to two fixed glaring points. A corporal in dress-blue uniform appeared in the doorway.

"Sergeant Timons here?"

Paul's angry eyes pinned on the marine a menacing stare that started the dress-blue uniform shaking.

"Yeah, asshole, your mission is accomplished."

"I am to escort you to the bridge."

"Lead the fuckin' way. I only let dress-blues walk in front of me. If dress-blues are walking around there ain't much." Paul hunched over the corporal and looked at him sharply. The corporal didn't want to turn his back on this marine. He hesitated then abruptly swung and walked out. Paul threw a towel around his neck and followed his escort, wiping the sweat from his face as he went. Eddie squeezed his arm as he passed.

"You're startin' to space, bro. Be careful."

"I wish I had the live rounds of ammo. I wish I wouldn't fuck up all the time." Paul was out the hatchway and taking long strides that kept him on the corporal's heels like a wolf. He stalked him all the way to the bridge. The corporal opened a door. A bright light reflected from wide plexiglass windows.

It was dark outside but the enormous number of lightbulbs burning in the bridge forced Paul to squint through his fatigue. He drew his head back and down against his shoulders like an animal trapped in the corner of a cage.

Paul did not straighten to attention though the bridge was filled with officers of assorted rank, both marine and naval. Paul heard the corporal announce his arrival. The dress-blue uniform quickly disappeared out the hatch.

Paul could make out Captain Pelham. His outline became more distinct. He was standing next to the battalion commander who stood beside the ship's captain, equal in rank to a full bird colonel in the marines. Pelham spoke first.

"Sergeant Timons, this is Lieutenant Colonel Jacobson." Pelham's head swiveled from Paul to the battalion commander. Paul's eyes conveyed flames coming from the pit of his heart. They seared Jacobson's eyes and Jacobson did not like it.

"Don't you salute when you're in the company of officers, Sergeant?" Jacobson demanded in an immediate rush of authority.

Paul lifted his arm very slowly as if raising the barrel of a rifle and threw the salute at Jacobson. The battalion commander returned it.

Paul bent his knees like a football player in position for a tackle. His fuse had been burning rapidly toward its explosive content. Now it ignited with a burst that outshone the bright light of the bridge. With the detonation of his darkest impact his words flew like tracers into the bodies surrounding him.

"You assholes." He was seething. "You no good motherfuckers. You killed one of my men today. You set us up for an ambush then walked us right into it. Your whole fuckin' Marine Corps isn't worth Johnson's life."

Paul sprang from his haunches without another word. His mouth froze open in a silent chilling scream. His lips curled back from his teeth.

He went straight for the battalion commander with the detached vacancy of a warrior making his last stand. He sprang with the power of a god. His hands clawed the air and found Jacobson's throat before anyone had a chance to react. His hands closed on the throat with a vise-like grip that took Jacobson to the floor, snapping his ribbons off his uniformed chest and bulging his eyes. Paul locked his hands in a death-grip.

((He had the NVA soldier down and automatically positioned his thumbs to smash the windpipe. Adrenalin focused his two thumbs and they began the crushing motion that would kill the enemy soldier.))

Paul suddenly felt hands and feet punching and kicking him, wrapping around his throat, arms, hands and entire body until he was bearhugged down and had the wind knocked out of him.

He gasped and fought with all his strength against the six officers who were holding him down. He writhed and shook. His head struck the floor again and again but he didn't pass out. He began crying.

"Eh...eh...eh..." Paul's throat made no human sound. He strained one more time. The six officers could barely keep him down. He heard shouts above him, buttons popping and flying against walls, curses, voices berating him, then out of his mouth flew a scream that paralyzed them all.

The spasm of sound reverberated in the stunning impact of a single doomed man. Then words formed on his lips and squeezed out from the death-mask he had become.

"Oh God, please!" Then his eyes glazed over like those of a warrior cut down in a hail of fire.

A doctor rushed in and rammed a shot of Thorazine into his right leg. Paul felt nothing. He swooned in a spreading haze, emptied into the deepest caverns of thought. They carried him below decks into a more profound darkness.

He could feel them throwing him onto a berth. He heard Eddie's distant voice above the din. "What have you done to him!"

They buckled straps across his chest and waist and tied down his arms and legs. He rolled his eyes lazily in their sockets.

Paul closed his eyes on the bloodstained battlefield. He lay blasted into the barbed wire, the jagged points biting him in their grip. As he passed into unconsciousness he looked up once from the wire and saw an NVA soldier smiling down at him as he lifted his bayoneted rifle and rammed the spike down.

When he woke up groggy and faint the next day he could not tell what time it was. Impulsively he strained at the straps but gave up when he learned how tightly he was bound. He relaxed and took several deep breaths. The quarters were empty except for a naval officer sitting in a chair near him. The officer noticed that his eyes were no longer dilated or prismed but had the normal serene look of a twenty-year-old. Tears welled up and streaked down Paul's face.

"Who are you?" Paul asked. The words came from a swollen tongue and a throat full of glue.

"My name is Nelson," the officer said. "I'm a doctor. How do you feel this morning, Sergeant Timons?"

"Terrible, Doc, terrible."

"I should imagine so. You went through quite a struggle last night." Nelson smiled gently. His eyes were soft blue and relaxed. He sat in a chair with his legs crossed and leaned forward with his face cupped in his hands.

"Oh Jesus Christ, what did I do?"

"Well, Sergeant, you almost killed your battalion commander."

"What? No. Oh God."

"Do you feel in control now?"

"Yes, sir," Paul replied. "I didn't mean to hurt anyone." Paul started crying.

"It's alright to cry, Sergeant. Let it out. Don't be afraid. I'd like to unstrap you. Do you think I can?"

"Yes, sir," Paul said, swallowing hard.

"Good," the doctor said. "Like I told you, my name is Lieutenant Commander Nelson and I want to help you."

"Thank you, sir."

"I'm going to unstrap your legs first. Then we'll see how you feel, okay?" Nelson smiled.

"Yes, sir."

The doctor untied the straps securing Paul's legs, then sat back and observed him closely. Paul lifted his legs and stretched them.

"Feel any better?"

"Yes, sir."

"Now, Sergeant Timons, I'm going to unstrap one of your arms and give you a drink of water. Okay?"

"Yes, sir." With his free arm Paul reached out and took a glass of water from Nelson and drank it down. The water made it easier to talk.

"Now, before I unstrap your waist and other arm I want to talk to you for a few minutes." The doctor's voice was peaceful. "I want you to tell me exactly how you feel and what you remember of yesterday. Okay?" Nelson lifted a yellow legal pad, placed it on his lap and took out a pen.

"Well, sir," Paul began heavily, "I remember being on a patrol. I was walking point. We walked into an ambush. My men were being killed. I remember an emergency extraction. I remember a chopper. Then as soon as we got back to the basecamp we were overrun. Gooks everywhere. I couldn't stop them. They just kept coming. I couldn't stop the slaughter of my men." Paul shut his eyes tight.

"Open your eyes, Sergeant," Nelson said. "It's very important that you keep your eyes open and focused on me. Okay?" Paul opened his eyes. Nelson continued. "I want you to know that you are not in Vietnam. We are aboard a helicopter aircraft carrier called the Guam and we are off the coast of North Carolina. Do you understand?" Paul looked at him questioningly. "Do you believe me, Sergeant?"

"Yes, sir. But, then, I don't remember. Sir, I mean, what happened to me?" Paul was frightened.

"Well, Sergeant, you lost control. I'm not really sure why. I'm trying to find out. I want to help you."

"Did I hurt or kill anyone?"

"No, Sergeant. Your battalion commander has a sore neck, but he'll be okay." Nelson was choosing his words carefully.

"What was I doing then, sir? I remember men dying. NVA soldiers. An ambush. Being overrun."

"You are not in Vietnam, Sergeant. You must understand this fully and clearly. We are conducting operations off the coast of North Carolina. There was an accident. One of the men in your squad apparently drowned. When you were brought back to this ship you were taken to the bridge so your battalion commander and your captain could find out what happened. You lost control and attacked your battalion commander. Is that clear?"

"Yes, sir, I understand. I'm in a world of trouble." Paul had regained his senses and control and Nelson was aware of it. Paul continued. "I guess I'm going to the brig then, sir. I guess I'm headed for a dishonorable discharge. I guess I really fucked up this time."

"I don't know about that, Sergeant. I spoke with your commanding officer, Captain Pelham. He seemed quite concerned. It didn't appear that he wanted you punished. You only have four months left, is that correct?"

"Yes, sir. Four months left on a four-year hitch. I'd like to go home with an honorable discharge. I fought hard for my country but, sir, I wish, I wish..."

"Continue, Sergeant, please." Nelson's head was down and he was writing something on the yellow pad. He lifted his head and looked at Paul.

"I wish there was no Vietnam. No country, no war, I wish it were over so I could go home." Paul looked at the ceiling. "I think I'm crazy. I'm gone and it makes me scared."

"No, Sergeant, I don't think you're crazy. Your service record book is impressive. You were an honor graduate out of Parris Island. Meritoriously promoted to sergeant. You received decorations any marine would be proud of. High pro and con marks. Excellent fitness reports as a sergeant. But I do believe you may be suffering from what doctors termed in other wars 'shellshock.' Do you know what that is?"

"Yes, sir, I understand. You lose it. You can't control yourself anymore."

"I don't want you to be scared, Sergeant. I want you to be aware of it at all times. I want you to pay particularly close attention to what you're feeling. At all times." Nelson continued. "I've seen it in vets, most markedly in those who've been in a lot of combat. On the mainland I've worked with some vets who were at Hue City. One vet of Hue was only in Vietnam for a week and a half and was wounded three times. He saw most of his company wiped out. Can you imagine, Sergeant, a week and a half? He's getting a medical discharge and I don't know what the future will hold for him. The way I look at it you have two options. One is a medical discharge. The other is to be aware of your feelings at all times, try to control them and finish your four months. What do you think, Sergeant?"

"I think I'd like to finish my four months, sir."

"Good. I'd like to see the same thing. I'm going to release you now and have you flown back to the mainland. I will give you my office location and phone number at the infirmary at Camp Lejeune where I work. I want you to get in touch with me if you feel you are losing control. Okay? I'm also going to request that you be transferred out of your unit and placed in a transients' barracks with other short-timers. There'll be good food and light work. I don't think you should be in the field anymore. Do you agree to that, Sergeant

Timons?"

"Yes, sir. But I don't want to leave my partners. What about my partners, sir?"

"I don't want you around your unit anymore. I want you to stay put. I want you to go back to your barracks, pack your gear and stand by to move. You'll be with other short-timers from 'Nam. You guys understand each other. Okay?"

"Yes, sir. Can I say goodbye?"

"No, you will go back to the mainland. Is that clear?" Nelson bent over and untied Paul. He watched for several minutes while Paul stood up and stretched. Nelson was satisfied.

"Pack your gear, Sergeant, and go up to the flight deck. There's a chopper flying back to Cherry Point later this afternoon. You be on it. And stay in touch with me. Good luck, Sergeant." Nelson held out his hand and Paul shook it and saluted. Then Nelson turned and walked out.

On the flight deck Paul was alone with his thoughts. But he kept listening to two voices. One was Nicky Martinez' saying, "Paul Timons, what a horror...Paul Timons, what a horror..." The other was his own which kept saying, "The war must be stopped...the war must be stopped..."

Paul flew back to Cherry Point and caught a ride to Montford. Somehow he had survived again.

It was almost dark when he reached the little cubicle in the barracks. Only three days had elapsed since the sergeant-major had talked to him. He felt how each day ran sluggish and slow but in total abandonment. Each day in the Marine Corps was an endless realm of absurdity and madness. He had learned quickly never to question why but to do and to be ready to die. He saw himself as a punch-drunk fighter who had been mismanaged. At eighteen he was sent in to fight. His managers paid him the scantiest wages for his fights but told him he held the title. They made him defend it over and over again, no questions asked. They made him fight to the death. By his nineteenth birthday he was washed up, a pug, a young man who had gone over the ropes too many times. Paul felt finished. He did not feel beginnings, he felt ends.

Paul dropped his gear on the floor and left the barracks. He walked through the parking lot, past his "green-machine," then into the woods where the pines stood straight and high among their own shadows in the gathering twilight. He walked to where a limb lay outstretched, its branches upright. At its end he dug with his hands through layers of pine needles until he felt the soft earth. He dug into the loamy soil until his fingers touched a box. It was an ammo case that sealed tight against weather and moisture. He cracked the lid open and pulled out a bag of marijuana and some rolling papers.

He rolled six big bombers, stuck them in his pocket and reburied the box. He lit a joint and smoked it with deep inhales, holding each hit as long as he could until what was left was only a tiny pinprick of light.

He lay back and relaxed. "Man made booze, God made grass, who do you trust?" He felt happy. What a strange feeling raced through his body and mind now. He began laughing.

Still laughing, he walked out of the pine grove and across the parking lot to the "green-machine." He started it up and heard it purr beneath him. He backed it up and roared out of the parking lot, down the road and out the maingate.

On Route 285 he gunned the car to sixty and held it firm. He felt a great exhilaration. How anyone could take driving a car for granted was beyond him. It was the greatest freedom he could know. He rolled down the window and let the cool air blow rough on his face. He shoved a Dylan tape in the stereo, cranked it up and lit another joint. He let himself laugh some more. It felt strange. People were allowed to feel this?

Paul drove on, letting the drone of the car's engine hypnotize him. He got more and more stoned listening to Dylan's nasal voice.

"Man, we're flyin' now, Bobby," Paul said out loud.

He looked at the speedometer. It was racing past eighty miles an hour.

"I'm movin' free now and I could move free forever."

The highway fled beneath him, the lines zipping past like white strobe lights, the headlights bearing down on the night. He passed an outdoor movie theater. The film "Woodstock" was playing.

Paul braked hard, sending the car into a spin. He righted it, pulled the car onto the shoulder and, in one sweeping motion, fishtailed in a big U-turn and raced back to the drive-in.

By the time he found a place to park and pulled a speaker through the window, the movie was half over. Santana was blasting and Paul began rocking with joy in the car.

"Jesus, this is just the greatest movie I ever saw." He lit another joint. "Whoa there...you are getting stoned, Sergeant. Yes, sir, yes, sir!"

The groups jammed one after another and everybody in the film and the cars was bouncing up and down to the heavy beat. Paul felt he was in heaven.

The film was nearing its end. Paul's eyes widened to see it was almost over. In the movie people were beginning to leave the concert in shawls and rags like Vietnamese peasants. A new dawn rose above the hill leading to the stage. It was littered with debris like a battlefield.

Then Paul saw him.

Jimi Hendrix, the grunts' brother of the bunkers, at Con Thien, at Khe Sanh, stood before the ruin in a white tassled jacket and held in his hands not a machine gun but a white Stratocaster guitar. He began to play. Paul scrunched down in his seat and stared with unblinking eyes at the lean black man. Using no vocals, Hendrix began his rendition of "The Star Spangled Banner."

Hendrix's guitar became as big as the war and their entire generation. The man became larger, his huge hands playing over the strings, his face a mask of sorrow, anguish and loss. Those great hands played over the strings, at times caressing, at times contorting, and his face responded to what the strings said.

Hendrix rose to a sacred playing, racing up and down until he came to "the rockets' red glare" and "the bombs bursting in air." Here he twisted and wrenched the guitar strings. The instrument cried out in pain, bombs rained down and exploded through the banks of amplifiers and speakers. Universal agony screamed out of the strings until the final bursts of sound tore forth.

Hendrix jumped into "Purple Haze," singing especially hard on the line "Is it tomorrow or just the end of time?" As the movie faded Hendrix played a slow dirge and you saw him no more. Only the last sad song.

"That song should be played in every school auditorium, before every baseball game this government and nation will ever witness," Paul said out loud.

It was past midnight when Paul returned to the barracks. He fell onto his bunk with a great numbness in his body, his ears ringing and his heart full of a joy he had never known.

He did not get up for reveille the next morning. He slept in. The barracks was empty because the unit was still on maneuvers. It felt good to be alone and able to stretch in the sack and doze again. He looked at his watch and discovered that it was 10 a.m. He rolled over and tried to sleep some more. Then the door banged open and slammed shut. He sat right up, open-eyed. It was Staff Sergeant Harris.

"Well, sweet pea, I see you're enjoying life," Harris said.

"Doctor Nelson told me to rest," Paul replied.

"Oh yeah, you rest. The entire Marine Corps works and you rest. You're our very own special case, a sweet pea sergeant."

"What do you want, Sergeant Harris?"

"Well, Timons, they sent me back to cut your orders for the rest home. I have to fuckin' baby-sit your ass and be your fuckin' butler at the same time. Now, isn't that just great?"

Paul narrowed his gaze at Harris and Harris glared back. The staff sergeant stood in utilities near the door, his face reddening, and kept balling both his hands into fists as if he were squeezing something.

"First thing I want you to do is get the fuck out of the sack. Can you do that, sweet pea?" Harris was breathing heavily. Paul jumped out of bed. He was naked except for his white skivvy shorts. Harris smiled.

"You know," Harris began, "you remind me of when I was a DI at Parris Island. You look just like a boot piece of shit standing there. Do you have any idea how many boot pieces of shit I had to put up with? Try to make marines out of them? It was an impossible job with shits like you. I endured it for almost two years. Can you imagine, sweet pea, how many sorry shits were assigned to me? Hundreds of 'em. Thousands of 'em. About wanted to make me puke. And now I end up with you. Now that's justice, eh?"

Paul said nothing. He was forgetting everything Doctor Nelson told him. A low voice from deep in his gut was growling in his throat. It filled his head and body and looked out from his eyes. Harris continued.

"Sergeant, I had a long talk with Captain Pelham. I mean, you tried to tear our battalion commander's head off. That alone just pisses me off to no end. The captain sent me back to cut your orders and chauffeur you to the rest home. I think you should get yours, you know what I mean? Anyway, the Corps ain't what it used to be. Captain Pelham said this is the way it is. I think it sucks. But he did say that if you fucked up again appropriate action would be taken against you. Now, that's fair, isn't it, sweet pea?" Harris's eyes spread open and a sneer came across his lips. "I'm gonna take you to the rest home but we're gonna do it my way. Do you understand my way?"

"Anything you say, Harris," Paul responded.

"Atten-*hut*!" Harris shouted. Paul assumed the position of attention by his bunk, his eyes straight ahead. Like boot camp again. Harris was the drill instructor. He walked over to Paul, his face inches away. As he spoke his mouth threw spit.

"You will, puke, get showered and shaved and put on your uniform. Then you'll stand a junk-on-the-bunk inspection just for me. Do you UNDERSTAND, sweet pea? EVERYTHING will be in order. Can you do that? Do I have to hold your hand? If so, of course I'll do everything I can to help. You will not fuck up again. You will leave here a marine or you won't leave here at all. I just fuckin' can't stand shits like you. You make me so goddamn fuckin' mad. How you make me mad!" Harris was boring into Paul's eyes and throwing more spit. "You will answer everything I say with an 'aye, aye, sir' and salute. Got it, sweet pea? HAVE YOU GOT IT, SWEET PEA!" Harris's hands were rolled into tight fists and, without warning, he punched Paul.

((The sound came from somewhere above. "Mortars!" Jimmy screamed and squatted, pressing himself in on Paul. Crunch! Crunch! Crunch! The rounds came down on top of them across the perimeter of the fire-support base. Crisp detonations cracked the earth, splintering, whizzing, mixed with screams. The mortar fire rained down on them for ten minutes. "Fuckin' bastards!" Jimmy screamed. Then the mortars stopped. Instantly long explosions, rising in white-heat flashes, ran like a fuse through the wire. "Fuckin' bangalore torpedoes. Up, Paul. We're fuckin' bein' overrun!"

Jimmy sprang up and laid the bipod in front of the fighting hole and poured a stream of bullets into the wire. Paul came up next to him. But, somehow, it wasn't Paul. Paul was strangely high and screamed like a beast, adrenalin bursting through his body in successive waves. Like a dark god Paul pulled the trigger of his M-14 full automatic and held the recoil rigid so his aim did not falter. He ejected the magazine. "Down, Jimmy," he said.

Paul squatted, fumbled for another magazine, rammed it in his rifle, then crisscrossed two bandoliers of ammo across his chest. He came up firing. "Down," said Jimmy.

Paul could not see directly in front of him, but out of the corners of his eyes he could detect enemy soldiers, many of them, running and firing and coming through the breaches of the wire. The first wave of enemy soldiers was already beyond the wire. "Holy Christ, Holy Christ, Jimmy, there's a million of the fuckers!" Jimmy came up wide-eyed and firing with a vicious rage.

The first wave to come through was a company of sappers, explosive experts with homemade satchel charges strapped to their chests or slung across their shoulders. They lunged and dove into any fighting hole they could. "Sappers!" Jimmy screamed as the dark-pajamed enemy began diving into holes, grabbing marines in a death embrace and blowing the satchel charges.

Illumination rounds were popping above the wire and coming down dangling from their parachutes. But the fog was too thick and it wasn't until they were ten feet from the ground that anything could be seen, and then only a quick photograph of someone moving.

NVA Army regulars began pouring through the breaches, mixing with the first units of sappers. Jimmy turned and fired a burst. A sapper snapped back, pulling the string on his satchel charge. The explosion ripped open the air ten feet from their position. Shrapnel cut into Jimmy's right shoulder and neck and tore off an ear. "Christ, I'm fuckin' hit, the cocksuckers finally got me!" Jimmy still leaned into his weapon sending out fire.

Paul's rifle kicked ferociously against his shoulder until his entire arm and chest were numb from the recoils. Screams were rising from both sides.

An overhead view of the battlefield would show it now littered with dead North Vietnamese who had barely made it through the first line of the marines' defense.

Paul saw on his left a machine gun barrel glowing red, the steady stream of bullets and tracers unstopping and the marine braced against it unstoppable.

The NVA kept coming in waves. Illumination rounds descended, giving an eerie glow to the slaughter. "Fix bayonets!" Jimmy screamed through his wounds. Paul and Jimmy seated their bayonets on the end of the barrel, their fingers burning from the heat of the metal as they snapped the blades in place.

Four NVA in khaki uniforms and pith helmets came at them. A burst hit the dirt in front of Paul, stinging his eyes. He fell back in the hole. Jimmy prepared to meet them. With only ten rounds left in his rifle he could drop only two of them. "Shit! Fuck!" Jimmy roared.

He leapt out of the fighting hole, lying exposed, and sprang on the other two. Paul, his rifle emptied, also jumped. They each took on one of the enemy, smacking rifle against rifle, slashing bayonets.

Paul knocked over the soldier nearest him and drove his bayonet through the enemy's throat. The blade went through like butter. The soldier went into a spasm and frothed blood. Jimmy received a second wound from a bayonet rammed in his thigh. Paul jumped to his aid, hearing the crunching of snapped bone and ligament as he thrust his bayonet again and again. Paul lifted Jimmy and carried him back to their hole. "We're fucked," Jimmy said sleepily.

The machine gun had stopped firing and the courageous gunner was slumped over his hot and smoking weapon. He appeared dead. An enemy soldier unloaded a burst in his back and the gunner's body jerked forward with the impact.

Paul fired at the soldier. He blew over and fell in the hole with the dead gunner. "Put your back against mine, Paul, we each got one hundred and eighty degrees to cover." Jimmy was getting weak from loss of blood. More soldiers came on them.

Suddenly Jimmy was out of the hole again, growling after an enemy soldier. But his leg wound caused him to fall. He lay face down cursing each time an enemy bayonet struck him in the back. Frantically switching magazines and firing, Paul leapt from the hole and ran to Jimmy. Dragging him back, he knew he was dead. There was an explosion.

Paul's left leg was punched out from under him and he fell. With great effort he got Jimmy back to the hole. They fell in, Jimmy's body landing on top of Paul.

Two enemy soldiers raced by and peered in. They fired into the back of Jimmy's head. They missed Paul. Jimmy's brains splattered against Paul and hot tissue stung his eyes. His face was covered with Jimmy's blood.

When Paul raised his head once more his face had changed forever. Brain tissue mixed with blood stuck on his face like leeches. Paul was no longer a mortal man. He was a god anointed by the dead.))

Let It Be

My six-man recon team is settled into its night defensive position. We call this spot a "harbor site" and it is usually located on the highest ground that is near us during our day's patrolling. Several hours before dusk we lie quietly in an ambush, and when the darkness begins to envelope us so our human outlines cannot be made out from the rest of the jungle topography, we move up and settle in.

On this patrol we are near the Laotian border within two kilometers of the Ho Chi Minh trail and intelligence told me before we set out that the North Vietnamese were moving at least a regiment, and perhaps an entire division, down irregular roads they cut under the triple canopy jungle. Unable to spot them from the air, they dispatched the six of us to do the job.

I am the pointman and Corporal Becker is the team leader. He walks directly behind me and behind him walks our radio operator, Lance Corporal Spiget. Behind Spiget is our corpsman, Doc Blanchard. Behind Blanchard walks our M-79 man, PFC Johnson, and behind Johnson is our tail-end charlie, Corporal Bates. We are the formidable Marine Corps force dispatched against a regiment, perhaps a division, of heavily armed enemy soldiers. On point I feel like a kamikaze pilot diving at an entire fleet of ships, but this is the job I've been trained to do and I do it well. We all have our jobs and it's all over, that quick!

It's now 2 a.m. and we are on fifty-percent alert, which means that three of us are awake while three sleep. We are in a tight circle with seven-foot-high elephant grass around us. We can't see out anywhere around, so we depend solely on our hearing. I'm leaning into my rucksack while lying on the ground, the barrel of my M-14 rifle pointing towards the Laotian border. It's been quiet until now, but I'm beginning to pick up frightening sounds. I hear the

VAROOM of truck engines and the metallic grinding of gears being shifted. My heart begins pounding its way up through my ears. Trucks! Many trucks are beginning to move through to the east. I turn to Becker.

"Hey, Beck, you hear that shit!"

"Yeah, Paul, I got it!" he whispers back.

Becker immediately whispers to Spiget to wake up the rest of the team. He does this in silence and all six of us hunch into our weapons, listening. The trucks are much closer than two kilometers away and moving toward us. Soon we can make out voices. Goddamn, it sounds like they're everywhere around us! Spiget covers the radio handset so the crackle of transmissions is diminished. VAROOM. Grinding of gears being shifted, voices in the dark close and getting closer.

Bates is nervous and doesn't think he has a round chambered in his rifle. He pulls the bolt back and tries to slide it forward. Click!

"Quiet, you motherfucker!" Becker whispers.

The click is all it took. Within minutes we hear the movement of enemy soldiers around us. Becker leans toward me.

"I think we're fucked."

Except for my heart beating, I'm detached. I've been doing this and waiting for over ten months. I'm not surprised, my jaw opens and I breathe a steady rhythm through my mouth. The voice inside my head keeps saying "Oh shit! Oh shit! Oh shit!" nothing more. I take up the slack on the trigger of my rifle and wait. I hear branches breaking around us and the sinister sound of canvas cloth scraping and moving against branches. They're near us but don't know exactly where we are. Now the game starts and the voice in my head changes. "Come on, you fuckers! Come on! Come on!" Spiget turns the radio off. Another click. The movement around us stops. The silence weighs a ton.

"Dou mow wee, dou mow wee." A North Vietnamese voice floats across from the east. My team lies frozen. I breathe now with great difficulty, holding every other breath like I'm going deep under water.

Tap...tap tap. Tap...tap tap. Less than thirty meters away to the east. Tap...tap tap, tap...tap tap, the signal returned from our north.

The North Vietnamese soldiers are talking to each other by clicking sticks together. They want us to open fire and give away our position. They're still not sure where we are. Tap...tap tap, twenty meters away, to the east again! My team doesn't move a muscle, we all hold our breath.

Suddenly a small hard object, about the size of an orange, is hurled into the middle of us. It goes "thunk" as it hits and rolls to my feet. I do not think, not even for a moment. I turn, grab the object with my right hand and draw it to my body. I press it with both hands into my gut, curl myself on top and grit my teeth. One second passes. I clutch my eyes tight and my face becomes the grimace of a death mask. My life does not pass before me. Two seconds. I am trying to kill myself from the inside before the explosion. Three seconds. I feel so helpless I want to scream. Four seconds. The voice inside my head does not speak, but my eyes are wide open already seeing my guts pour out of me on the ground. Five seconds. Time to die. Six seconds.

My fingers begin to move against the object, feeling its texture. Seven seconds. The voice inside my head begins to speak. "It's not smooth like a hand grenade, it's bumpy like a rock." Eight seconds. I lift my right hand. It *is* a rock! They're still not sure where we are. For they too are sometimes confused by a night of jungle sounds. Nine seconds. I hand the rock to Becker and he passes it silently around to the other team members. No one fires. Discipline! Discipline! Discipline!

Tap...tap tap. Tap...tap tap. Moving farther away from us now. Receding down along the small ridge we're on. The sound of cloth scraping against brush more distant. Tap...tap tap. Eighty meters away. "Dou mow wee!" A hundred meters away. Tap...tap tap. We can barely hear them. They're gone.

I am waking up out of an abyss. What the fuck! I'm strapped to a table in an otherwise empty room and when I lift my head and strain my eyes I can see a heavy wood and steel door with a small window and a face peering in at me. I drop my head back, forcing my eyes to stay open.

The walls, floors and ceiling of this room are bare and are

painted a dull blue, a numbing blue, a throbbing, aching blue. There must be another window behind me that leads off the tenth story of this Veterans Administration Hospital, because a stiff shaft of sunlight strikes the room.

My arms, trunk and legs are all strapped down tightly. I feel pain all over, but especially in my right thigh where the needle of Thorazine was stabbed in. My mouth feels like it's full of cotton. They've snared me again, goddamn them for strapping me down. I strain hard but the restraints only seem to get tighter.

The door clicks from a key being turned, and opens. Doctor John Wallace walks in. I recognize him immediately.

"Feeling better, Paul?"

"Yeah, Doc, fine. Untie me, will ya?"

"Well, first I want to talk to you, make sure you're in control." He's smiling.

"I'm fine I tell you. Why you got to always strap me down and shoot me up with Thorazine?"

"It's for your own protection, we don't want you to hurt yourself." Not smiling. I hate these games.

"What do you want to know, Doc?"

"You've been out of it, Paul, for almost four hours. What do you remember of it?"

"I don't know. Maybe some gooks around and branches tapping and rocks being thrown."

"Well, that's interesting. Why do you think those three particular events were in it?" Concerned look. Professional. Doc Wallace leans forward and frames his face with his hand. He looks at me steady.

"What the hell, Doc, that's 'Nam."

"Gooks, branches tapping, rocks being thrown? Do you really feel in control now, Paul?"

"Yeah, Doc, no shit, lemme up. I hurt all over."

He unstraps only my legs first and allows me to stretch them. My arms and body remain bound. He chats with me a few more minutes, but I've turned him off. I only answer "yes" and "no" to his questions.

Finally I feel the restraints loosening around me and I sit up.

Whoa, the way back is so painful! Doc calls for an attendant to help me back to my room and he helps me lie down in bed.

"Drink this, Paul, it'll help you sleep." He's barely audible. He holds a small plastic medicine cup in his hand. He motions to me with it.

"What's this?" I ask.

"Some liquid Trilafon." Another tranquilizer. I drink it down and lie back to sleep. It comes so hard. Been this way for twenty years. Life is a long roar. Always surrounded. The enemy has to know exactly where you are or they'll spend all their time trying to find you. On what you show depends your survival. I hear movement around my bed. Sounds like feet marching. Listening, I slide off the chasm and move...

"The fuckers are all around us!" Becker leans his camouflaged face next to mine and whispers the urgency. I take up the slack on the trigger of my rifle and wait...

CEREMONY OF THE BEAST

He is come, this beast,
This killing machine!
I have seen him reared up,
Neck hairs bristling.

This is his pleasure
And he thrives
In his barren
Existence.

His release
Feeding in the merciless
Slaughters that mar
Our times.

Primordial with fear
Dealing death blows
To keep himself near
To himself.

There he stands!
In my conscious self
With all the grim drippings
Of mankind

Scaled over his
Whole being.
Weighting him in
Horror.

Gnawing, gnawing
At the edge
Of his age
Crouched and ready.

I see him advancing!
Violent death pulling hard on his time,
His desperate life
Without meaning.

He sees me
In the blood blue clouds
Bruised across
The face of his eyes.

And he is always with me.
With me
Who turns to sand
Whittled away by these ancient winds

Of this epic mass—
Hear my prayer.
My name is but a monument
Before his fiery passage!

He howls from the cavernous pinnacle of his heart.
From his wounded eyes he hurls his rage.
And the whole century shakes!

EPILOGUE

The moment I became a complete pacifist I was on a patrol in the Khe Sanh Valley. We had just implanted a string of three sensor devices and made a lot of noise. I was sitting on my rucksack, head bent, facing the burning heat of my exhaustion. I couldn't blink my eyes fast enough to keep the sweat out, or the sharp stinging.

I looked up.

You see, the NVA had adopted a new battle tactic. They called them "spotter teams." Realizing marine recon teams were their most dangerous enemies because of abilities to sniper them, call in artillery, and not be seen, they decided to make teams themselves. These "spotter teams" were made up of four or five men each. Just like us. That day in the middle of that withering hostile valley I sat warily with only three other men. Our faces and hands and arms were camouflaged. And except for our eyes, we looked like deadly little pieces of bushes sneaking about. The "spotter teams" dressed the same as us. Their faces and hands and arms were camouflaged, and they wore American jungle utilities. They carried M-16 rifles. Their sole job was to hunt us.

I focused my eyes.

Twenty meters from me I saw a piece of bush squatting. What gave him away was when he reached up to wipe the sweat from his eyes. What also gave him away was when he lifted his M-16 and aimed it at me. My rifle lay across my lap.

I looked into his eyes.

He didn't fire! They were trying to surround us. I stared into his eyes. His reflection wavered. I wiped the sweat from my eyes.

He looked at me.

I gripped my rifle tight and went for it! Squeezing off rounds even as I brought the barrel up. His eyes still seemed to register surprise before the mirror shattered.

I took point and led the team out the back door. I moved out at almost a run, frantically switching magazines so I'd have a fresh one. I gritted my teeth and burst through.

"All right! I'm coming right at you and right through you!" I seethed.

Luckily they hadn't had time to surround us. I tumbled into a bomb crater and the rest of the team followed. We set up our defense, radioed in choppers, and were pulled out.

I don't know, something about looking into my own eyes and killing myself.

War is every combatant's suicide.

I guess I finally looked around and saw that all of me was dying.

I remember just before I killed him I was thinking of the freedom everyone in America enjoys. I mean the ability to walk safely to the first ice cream store and order a thick shake. I'm talking on the level that counts. It was so damn hot I was thinking if I made it home I'd never take that for granted again.

But in war even the simplest of thoughts are shot.

I smelled the flowery grays. I was just a young void then. I'm a pacifist now. With a bullet through his brain.

You see, I've left my blood on both sides of the ocean. In Vietnam and in America.

In Vietnam on a dark night in Tet, 1969, when we were overrun. In America on a wall in the red-line brig at Camp Lejeune, North Carolina. Two staff sergeants were pounding my head against it. I remember what they were saying.

"Admit you're a communist!"

I admitted it, but I never considered myself one.

You see, at first I gritted my teeth just to spite them. By the fourth or fifth blow my nose was bleeding and my head really hurt. Pain makes you agree to many things.

I know the nightly nightmares that unravel like a long war novel with all the camera angles just right. All the perfect images of the slaughter. More than any director or screenwriter could ever conjure.

I know how you never shake walking point. It's how you move through the supermarket. It leads you into restaurants and bars. How it takes you home at night. It's terrible stalking! How my skin would crawl!

I know the rigorous battling pinned down in flashbacks. The terrible sounds! The coughing that is choking blood! The drowning!

I know how it feels, while this is going on, to be jumped by hospital attendants and forced down. My arm bent up hard behind my back with a screech of pain. A hard, heavy forearm crushed against my throat.

I know how it feels, while this is going on, to see the needle of Thorazine lifting and falling like a great wave. The solstice of pain when the point struck. The humiliation of it. The seeming insensitivity to what I was going through.

I know what the bed in the seclusion room feels like. The white belts with the locking silver buckles. Strapped down like a monster created by a mad scientist. The fear in bringing the dead back to life.

Always at that point, before the Thorazine took its heavy syrup effect on my mind, I would have a final flashback of being a prisoner of war. And as I lost consciousness I would see myself being punished for trying to escape.

Now I know I must live with the war novels and read them as such. Disengage myself from the scenes and make like I'm reading, say, Hemingway or Remarque.

I don't have any more uncontrollable flashbacks. I catch myself at the beginning of one and say, wow, here comes another one of those *Books on Tape* audio cassettes, accompanied by a VCR and videotape in technicolor by panavision! Starting to ring through my head like I have the headphones of a walkman on!

I sit right down at my typewriter. Or pick up a pencil and some paper, and get ready for the volume to be cranked up.

I write it all down, fast as it comes. I only ask everyone to get the hell out of my way! I tame it so it can never tame me.

I don't mind sleeping at night. I know I must see that which I survived and am a witness to. Because, the price of these visions is that one lives to see.

I don't mind walking point. It's the safest way to travel in this dangerous postmodern world. It's a gift! I treat it as such.

I go back to the hospital once in a while to say hello to everybody. They were doing their best with a very difficult encounter on their hands. I imagine those people were as scared as I was. I'm especially grateful there are people like that around trying to help us. Caring the best they can while they try to deal with their own mortal wounds. I try to bless them with my hugs. They've earned that.

I don't know how much time I have left. Or any of us for that matter. A novel? A novella? A short story perhaps? I hope it's more than a poem...Only a haiku? Damn! I gotta get to work!

I am I and the voice is me. It is this voice of me that speaks. "Me" finds its own pace when I hear it. I only listen. When I talk it doesn't come out right. So I write it down. The only life is the life of a writer. Who said that? Upright now...